# Hamble to
# Helsinki *and beyond*

*Fay and Graham Cattell*

Adlard Coles Nautical
London

Published 2001 by Adlard Coles Nautical
an imprint of A & C Black (Publishers) Ltd
35 Bedford Row, London WC1R 4JH
www.adlardcoles.co.uk

Skipper's Cruising Guide Series: Copyright © Fred Barter 2001
Copyright Book 3 © Fay and Graham Cattell 2001

ISBN 0-7136-5896-7

A CIP catalogue record for this book is available
from the British Library.

Typeset in 10pt Palatino
Printed in England by
The Cromwell Press

# CONTENTS

**CRUISING**
**ASSOCIATION**

*During this cruise, extensive use*
*was made of the* Cruising Association
Handbook, *now in its eighth edition; an*
*invaluable source of information compiled by*
*CA members and based on their personal*
*experiences when cruising.*

*For more information contact:*
*The General Secretary*
*CA House*
*1 Northey Street*
*Limehouse Basin*
*London E14 8BT*
*Tel: 020 7537 2828*

W E FIRST VISITED THE BALTIC IN 1995 - the year we were both retired and able to take long cruises. In that year we sailed from England and reached Stockholm by July but then realised it was time to start the journey home - three weeks of paradise in the Göta Canal was some compensation. We promised ourselves that we would return but next time overwinter somewhere to give ourselves time to explore without worrying about the return journey.

In 1996 we sailed round Britain and the next year had only a six-week cruise - much of the summer being lost whilst moving house.

By 1998 we felt it time to return to the Baltic. By then we had joined the Working Group organising the Cruising Association's Baltic Millennium Rally and had undertaken to carry out research - which also continued during our 1999 and 2000 cruises. Thus, in 1998 our plan was to sail to Helsinki via Estonia and overwinter the boat somewhere in the Baltic. First we had a "shakedown" cruise to France leaving us the opportunity to return home should anything vital, have been left behind. Persistent contrary winds in May sent us inland through the Dutch canals, even through Dokkum, something we had previously been told was impossible for a boat with our draught. We experienced every type of weather except snow - there was only one short period of high pressure but poor weather did not stop our achieving our goal. We visited Latvia briefly, sailed through Estonia and by 12th July reached Helsinki where we stayed several days. Our journey then took us through the Finnish Islands to Åland and back to Sweden's Stockholm archipelago where we found the ideal place to overwinter.

This is the story of that voyage, but we have also included extracts from our cruise logs of the succeeding two summers - years when we have spent much more time exploring and getting to know all three Baltic States, their harbours, their people - and travelling across country by bus, train and hire car. We visited 10 countries, coped with 10 other currencies and at least nine languages. Our journey lasted five months and we logged 2,487NM. The log of this cruise was a joint winner of the CA's Hanson Cup in 1999. There is not room in this little book to tell you everything but the full logs of all our cruises are available in the CA Library.

We have sailed together, just the two of us, since the days we learned to sail in dinghies in the south of France - some thirty years ago. Apart from the pleasure of friends' company for weekend sailing during the days when we were working we have never had any crew, nor felt the need of them, even when the going has been tough. Thus we avoid the deadlines of having to be at specific ports at specific times to meet up and are never lacking company - there are fellow sailors, and even some landlubbers, of every nationality in our circle of friends.

In the days when we "had to be at work on Monday morning" we still managed to sail off the Scottish West Coast and the English East Coast with a trailer-sailer, and later made many trips to France, the Channel Islands and to the Netherlands. The present TAM O'SHANTER - a Beneteau First 38S5 - is our fourth cruiser. She may be a surprising choice for a semi-liveaboard life but for us she combines our passion for fast exciting sailing and provides the space to move around in comfort below.

TAM O'SHANTER is still at Bullandö in Sweden during the winters - it may be some time before she returns to tidal waters!

### River Hamble

50°52'.84N/01°17'.84W  to Studland Bay: 50°38'.75N/01°56'.02W  – 40NM

## Wednesday 22nd April

We were launched on Monday and, between downpours, have been loading and packing away ever since. Just after 1100 we leave the pontoon at Swanwick Marina, motor down river and out into the Solent. There is some sunshine, a south east breeze later veering southerly, strange cloud formations over the Isle of Wight then a sudden squall catches us going through Hurst Narrows - omens of what is to come?  Studland appears peaceful and sheltered and we drop anchor for the  night. Will our shakedown cruise to France start soon?

## Thursday 23rd to Sunday 26th April  – 24NM

For four days we shelter from strong south to south westerly winds, moving between Studland, Swanage and South  Deep (Poole Harbour).  We make some shore trips and get used to the new timetable for Shipping Bulletins regretting the demise  of  the station reports on the daytime broadcasts.

*Mouth of the River Hamble*

**Studland to Cherbourg**

49°38'.74N / 01°37 '.33W – 66NM

## Monday 27th April

At last a favourable forecast - a light westerly. Anchor is weighed at 0600 but where is the wind? We motor two thirds of the way across the Channel before we pick up a breeze and can enjoy a pleasant sail in a westerly F3. The visibility is excellent - the English coast is still visible after 35 miles; the Cotentin Peninsular from about 25 miles off. The effect of today's massive spring tides is to increase the wind and we are reefing as we approach the coast. There is plenty of space in the visitor's berths and we are in time for a meal ashore. Later a strong N/NE sets in and keeps us in Cherbourg for a week.

## Tuesday 28th April to Sunday 3rd May

**Cherbourg**

It is easy to lose time when the weather is unsettled, but we have to take on the necessary provisions for a long cruise. The wind sets in from the north to north east and in the event we stay in Cherbourg. It is mostly bitterly cold and frequently rains. There are compensations - it is a French Public Holiday on 1st May and friends have come from Paris to visit their boat. The wind has blown Brits across the channel and we are delighted to find Gilly and Graham

> **CRUISING INFORMATION REPORT**
>
> *CHERBOURG*
>
> *Well sheltered harbour. Very large marina. Visitors berth on finger pontoons in south western part of harbour. Water and electricity. Toilets/showers in block at head of pontoon. Yacht Club bar/restaurant and Harbour Office in one building. All facilities in nearby town.*

Cherbourg - Basilica

(ADFIN) two spaces along the pontoon. We also make acquaintance with fellow CA member Bob Hull in (SUNSET H) and there are restaurants and the supermarket, and even after all these years more places to discover.

# CHERBOURG TO BOULOGNE

On Monday 4th May we are at last able to leave Cherbourg and make a passage to St. Vaast (26 NM) followed by an exciting sail - in a strong north westerly wind - to Le Havre (66NM) - where we again lose a day to weather.

### Le Havre to Dieppe

49°55'.67N/01°05'.01E – 60NM

*Thursday 7th May*

A great sail - with a southerly wind off the land the sea is flat. The coastal scenery is quite spectacular. As far as Cap d'Antifer the cliffs are "layer cake" but past the cape they become greyish chalk with a fringe of green grass, here and there a stain of red soil runs down the cliff face and there are arches and stacks. Tucked in between breaks in the cliffs are the little towns of Etretat and Yport. High above Etretat a tiny chapel shares the skyline with the aviators' monument. We pass Fécamp, the nuclear power station at La Palue and then St.Valéry en Caux. We have tide against us most of the day but a good wind. In a pleasant sunny evening we enter Dieppe and tie up in the marina only to discover everything is locked and we cannot get off the pontoons - to enjoy an excellent meal ashore we have to move the boat to a pontoon by the harbour office.

### Dieppe to Boulogne

50°43'.51N/01°35'.95E  48NM

*Friday 8th May*

The fishing fleet keeps going all night with attendant washes and noise. We leave early and have a marvellous sail to Boulogne passing the dune-lined coast of the Bay of the Somme. Avoiding the Seacat we make our way to the tiny crowded marina. Within minutes of arrival we are visited by the Gendarmerie Maritime - who say they need information in case of accident! Our plan is to return briefly to Dover (for personal reasons) so tomorrow's tides in the Dover Strait are checked during the evening.

**CRUISING INFORMATION REPORT**

*DIEPPE*

Marina in old ferry basin. Good shelter but subject to swell in on-shore winds. Finger pontoons. Water and electricity. Toilets and showers. All facilities in town.

**CRUISING INFORMATION REPORT**

*BOULOGNE*

Obey port entry signals. Small marina in innermost part of harbour beyond ferry terminal. Limited berthing for visitors. Finger berths. Water and electricity. Toilets and showers. All facilities in town.

# BOULOGNE TO DUNKERQUE (VIA DOVER)

## Boulogne to Dover

51°06'.65N / 01°19'.77E – 25NM logged (+ 5NM tide - measured distance 30NM)

### Saturday 9th May

Another fishing harbour - we are again woken by engines revving and washes slapping the hull. At first we have a reasonable wind - S F2-3 and the prospect of another pleasant sail. The visibility is not good but we can see the French coast for some time - of England there is no sign, just a line of haze. The tide is streaming up through the Dover Strait and carries us fast on our way. We are just across the Varne Bank when the wind starts to increase and continues to do so until we have F6 gusting 7. This coincides with dodging two ships in the west-going lane and the onset of fog. Now we know why we could not see England. All three reefs are hastily pulled into the main and much of the genoa is rolled away. We are actually sailing at 9.5kts. The radar detects the coast one mile away but it is hidden in the mist - we are nearly up the beach west of Dover before we see the wall - the seas are now horrendous reflecting back from the wall but with some help from the engine we manage to negotiate the western entrance - fortunately no ferries or hovercraft are moving and Port Control give us immediate clearance. Inside the wall the sea is calm but the wind still strong. The forces in the ether have not yet finished with us however -

> ### CRUISING INFORMATION REPORT
>
> #### DOVER
>
> Major port — entry/exit only with permission of Port Control (VHF Ch. 74). Choice of tidal basin or locked-in berths in either Granville or Wellington dock. Finger pontoons. Water and electricity. Showers, toilets and laundrette. All facilities in town about 1 mile.

as we motor towards the marina we do not see that the tail of one of the boom preventers has been swept overboard - this quickly seizes its chance and grabs our prop - the engine stops and we drift helplessly but manage to glide into the entrance of Granville Dock where we

*Dover - dried out alongside the wall*

catch hold of the gate. The lock gates are about to be closed, fortunately we are seen, the harbour launch is sent for and we are taken to a berth. The Harbour Master suggests we dry out beside the wall tomorrow - the launch will take us round. We remain in Dover a further two days - removing the rope is a five minute job but of course we have to wait for the tide to go down and come back - and the wind continues strong.

## Dover to Dunkerque

51°02'.98N / 02°21'.94E – 36NM

*Tuesday 12th May*

The tide is not in our favour until 1100. The visibility is "adequate" and the wind has eased to a N 3/4. We seem to be in greater danger from the vast number of cross-Channel ferries than the traffic going up and down the Dover Strait although in the east-going lane we have to heave to to avoid two of the three ships sighted. Reaching Dunkerque, we berth in the marina beneath the great smoking chimneys of local industrial plant.

**CRUISING INFORMATION REPORT**

*DUNKERQUE*

Sheltered marina on port hand side of entry channel. Subject to frequent washes. Finger pontoons. Water and electricity. Toilets and showers. All facilities in town at least 1 mile.

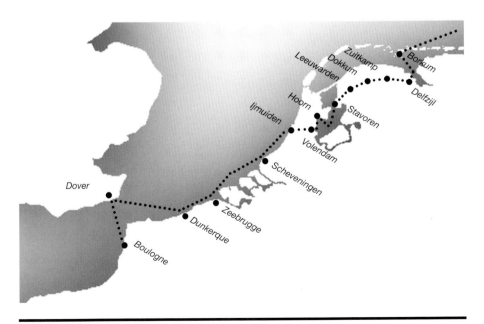

# DUNKERQUE TO STAVOREN

We now enjoy a period of more settled weather enabling us to make daily passages - Dunkerque to Zeebrugge (36NM), Zeebrugge to Scheveningen (70 NM) - with a stop for provisions and Dutch money, Scheveningen to IJmuiden, Seaport Marina (34 NM)

## Ijmuiden to Volendam

52°29'.62N / 05°04'.70E – 35 NM

*Saturday 16th May*

The forecast is again for N/NE wind, so to go inland via the IJsselmeer and Waddenzee appears the best option. We lock through to the Nord Zee Canal - how peaceful and pleasant in the canal, despite the industrial plant, the banks are grass and tree-lined - here swans and barges happily co-exist. A quick call into Amsterdam's Sixhaven marina and we pick up friends Jan and Ellemiek Schramp, for a day's sailing. The wind is NE F5/6 and we make a fast passage (in only 2.5m of water and a mass of yachts) to a crowded "touristy" Volendam where the shop keepers wear traditional costumes.

**CRUISING INFORMATION REPORT**

*IJMUIDEN*

Seaport Marina. Marina on starboard side after entering port breakwaters. Beware of strong cross-tide in entrance. Short finger pontoons with stem posts. Water and electricity (extra cost). Toilets and showers. Town some distance away — bus from gate. Very expensive by Dutch standards.

*Volendam, The Netherlands*

## Volendam to Hoorn

52°38'.20N / 05°04'.00E  – 10NM

### Sunday 17th May

The sun is shining and there are no tides. A pleasant sail to Hoorn where we anchor in 2m of water in the outer harbour - the birds are singing and above the treetops we can just see the tips of a windmill turning.

Next morning we move into the inner harbour and moor alongside staging. At the ANWB (Water Tourism Authority) office we are told there is definitely only 1.8m in the Dokkumer Groot Diep and we will not get through the canals to Delfzijl - very disappointing news but not surprising.

*Hoorn, The Netherlands*

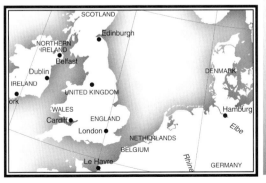

### Hoorn to Stavoren

52°52'.79N / 05°21'.90E – 38NM

## Tuesday 19th May

We tack up the Markermeer and lock through to the IJsselmeer at Enkhuizen. N/NE winds continue to be forecast and we put into Stavoren's south harbour, a place out of a story book - green banks

*Dutch Barge sailing the IJsselmeer*

with staging, little bridges and islands. A friendly goat is tethered on the bank but remembering the goat's habit of eating anything, I hope this one has not aquired a taste for mooring lines. The goat is taken away at nightfall so we can sleep in peace.

# THE FRIESLAND CANALS

### Stavoren to Leeuwarden

53°12'.22N / 05°46'.19E – 38NM

## Wednesday 20th May

Still the forecasts are for N/NE winds not allowing us to make progress outside the Frisian Islands so we decide to explore some of the Friesland Canals. From Stavoren we follow the Johan Friso canal, bordered by green meadows with black and white cows, and houses and barns with steep pitched roofs; then the Prinses Margriet Canal. We find ourselves in company with a Dutch yacht FLORYN and arrive at Leeuwarden together. The last bridge into the town is now shut and we tie up to a wall for the night.

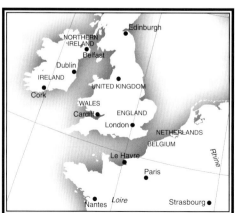

## Leeuwarden to Dokkum

53°19'.76N / 06°18'.54E – 14NM

### Thursday 21st May

*Dokkum - TAM O'SHANTER alongside FREJA - too shallow for us next to the bank*

The Bridge Master tells Pim ( the skipper of FLORYN) that boats of our size do go through the Dokkumer Groot Diep - the bottom is just soft mud - so we decide to take the gamble. As we progress through the Dokkumer Ee we find we have just enough water until we reach Dokkum where we run aground and have some difficulty but still manage to get through. We stay overnight in Dokkum, mooring alongside another boat - the water is too shallow beside the bank.

*Windmill at Dokkum - the shallowest water was found here*

15

## Dokkum to Zuitkamp

53°20'.25N / 06°18'.00E – 16NM

## *Friday 22nd May*

Dokkum is a very old and a surprisingly large town considering that all around are meadows and farms. We leave at midday and encounter no real problems - but much shallow water. We lock into the Lauwersmeer, have a little sailing in the Slenk and soon we are in a narrow channel leading to the open lock into Zuitkamp. In a rising wind we tie alongside a rusty fishing boat - but still have to pay harbour dues. Pim invites us to join his friends ashore at a Cornish Crabber association meet - thus we have a thoroughly enjoyable evening.

## Zuitkamp to Delfzijl

53°19'.00N / 07°00'.50E – 37NM

## *Saturday 23rd May*

We are awoken by a noise on the deck, sparrows with clogs on their feet looking for crumbs. By 0830 it is raining - real soaking rain

> **CRUISING INFORMATION REPORT**
>
> *DELFZIJL*
>
> *Large marina on south side of Eems estuary. Limited space for visitors. Finger pontoons. Water and electricity. Showers and toilets. All facilities in town.*

which gets in everywhere but we decide to continue to Delfzijl. Our route is via the Reitdiep which is much shallower than predicted, we are down to 2m at one place where the banks are being repaired. Passing through Groningen (which is the mast up route) there is a bridge every 20 yards and a strong stream carrying us along but a man on a bicycle keeps tearing ahead and opening the bridges. After Groningen we join the Eems canal which is much deeper - wide, straight and tree-lined. We have achieved what we have been told is impossible, to take a boat of our draught through the Dokkumer Diep. We take a day off in Delfzijl a little grid-system town protected from the sea by a high dyke.

## Delfzijl to Borkum

53°33'.52N / 06°45'.11E – 20 NM

*Monday 25th May*

The forecast is for W 4-5 and by midday, when we leave, the rain has stopped and the weather is brightening. In the event the wind is NW 3-4 right on the nose again so we tack down the Eems but the channel narrows between the sandbanks so we resort to motorsailing. At

**CRUISING INFORMATION REPORT**

*BORKUM*

*Visitors should proceed to Burkana which is in the main harbour. There is another marina on the port hand side of the entry channel but this is in a very run down state and is not recommended. Water and electricity. Showers and toilets. Town at other end of island 7 km distant.*

Borkum we pass the large marina which is still in a state of disrepair and has few occupants. We find the sailing club has taken over the whole of the Burkana harbour and shore facilities. The Harbour Master speaks excellent English, is very welcoming and the facilities are being improved.

## Borkum to Helgoland

54°10'.25N / 07°54'.00E – 75NM

*Tuesday 26th May*

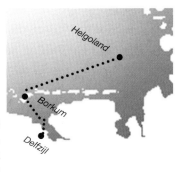

We have to work with the tides on this coast - thus we arise at 0400 and leave the harbour about 0430. It is a grey cloudy start threatening to rain. We can just see the lit buoys and motor sail through the channel. The wind is W3/4 - ideal for the day's journey but, as with all the Frisian Islands, the zeegat lies SE/NW. Finally we are clear of the island and its sand-banks and en route for Helgoland. We are not able to sail a course direct as there are shipping lanes along the coast - taking shipping to the Elbe, Jade and Weser rivers. We keep outside the lanes.

*Helgoland - fishermen's huts*

Around mid morning we are called on the VHF by a coastguard boat (here "coastguard" = marine police) then boarded by two officers who have excellent English and are very polite. We are told that we have infringed German regulations which require vessels to keep 1NM away from the shipping lanes. At first we are told we will be fined DM200 + costs but they later seem to change their minds about the whole matter and depart wishing us a good journey. We collect our wits and make all speed to Helgoland. *Note*: when we eventually returned home, we found the *Supplements to Macmillan's* awaiting us - Item 189.867 in reference to this TSS now adds a caution "The TSS immediately N of the ITZ and German Friesland Islands between Rivers Ems and Jade may not be crossed nor approached within 1M of the edge of the lanes, except in emergency or due to stress of weather. The German Water Police can impose on-the-spot fines or confiscate equipment to the value of DM2000, pending payment of the fine ...". *(It should be noted that this is a German rule, not an international rule - the International Collision Regs do not specify a distance.)*

Helgoland - the harbours

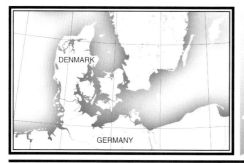

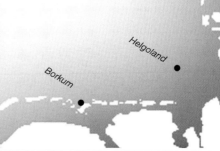

## Helgoland

18NM

### Wednesday 27th/Thursday 28th May

There is no reason weatherwise not to continue today but to get the tide right in the Elbe river would mean another crack of dawn start - so we stay a day. Helgoland was under British rule until it was "swapped" for Zanzibar in the 1890s. The buildings were all destroyed during WW2 and the island was used for RAF bombing practice until 1952 when it was finally returned to Germany. Therefore there are no original buildings and everything dates from after 1952. It is a rather unreal place - a duty--free haven where ferryloads of passengers come daily from the mainland.

On Thursday morning we depart at 0635 - there is a south easterly F2 on the nose, the visibility is hazy but adequate but after a few miles we run into thick fog and decide to turn back - we feel that even with radar, to risk the strong tides, buoys and shipping in the Elbe entrance (not to mention the police) is taking an unnecessary risk. The fog follows us back and is so thick that we cannot see the harbour entrance until we are there and even inside the harbour the fog is equally thick. Several boats have turned back; we help each other tie up and a bottle of Schnapps is passed round - everyone is so relieved to be safe and we quickly learn the German for fog. Needless to say, by the time we have lost the tide, the fog clears sufficiently to make a passage but it is too late for today. During the day a German boat comes alongside (you raft up in this harbour) and we get talking to Antje and Hobe Hein (SAVOIR VIVRE) and spend the evening together. Our impression on our previous visit was that the Germans were indifferent, our experiences this time are quite the opposite, everyone is most friendly and helpful, most willingly speak English and those who can't are still friendly and attempt communication.

*Helgoland's largest stack – called "Lange Anna"*

### CRUISING INFORMATION REPORT

#### *HELGOLAND*

*Large visitors' harbour - yachts raft out. No electricity. Office on opposite side of harbour.*
*Fuel (duty free) and water obtainable in Binnenhafen - motor out of yacht harbour, round E mole and follow buoyed channel. Fuel pontoon is located in SW corner of Binnenhafen. Self service - pay at chandlers on quay. Pump out station also in Binnenhafen.*

## Helgoland to Brunsbüttel

53°53'.28N / 09°07'.85E  –  51NM

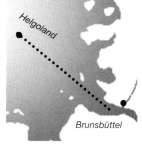

Brunsbüttel

### *Friday 29th May*

Overnight the east wind rose to F6 making the harbour very uncomfortable. By morning the wind has eased somewhat and we depart with two reefs in the main and the working jib. There are large and confused waves in the harbour entrance but once outside things quieten down a little. Gradually the wind drops away and the reefs are shaken out; the full genoa is hoisted but all to no avail - by the time we reach the Elbe Light Vessel we are motoring again to keep up with the tide in order to make Brunsbüttel before high water. We follow SAVOIR VIVRE and SNOWBIRD, and two German yachts we have met in Helgoland, across the shipping lanes feeling that there is safety in numbers but no gun boats are sighted today although various police boats are about on the Elbe river. With several other yachts we lock into the Kiel Canal remembering that the pontoons are almost at water level and we need to have our fenders very low. Once through, we turn into the little marina at Brunsbüttel - the Baltic is now only 98km away at the far end of the canal.

*Entering the Kiel Canal - the locks at Brunsbüttel*

> **CRUISING INFORMATION REPORT**
>
> ***BRUNSBÜTTEL***
>
> *Small marina on port hand side just beyond the locks into the Kiel Canal. Water and electricity available. Yachts berth alongside around the perimeter and raft out.*

# THE KIEL CANAL AND EIDER RIVER

## The Eider River

54°16'.35N / 09°18'.48E – 42NM

*Saturday 30th/Sunday 31st May*

We have learned of a yard in Rendsburg where it may be possible to overwinter - but with the weekend and Pentecost everything will be closed until Tuesday. We decide to spend the intervening time exploring the Eider River which connects the North Sea with the Kiel Canal. We leave the Kiel Canal at Gieselau. There are two locks near this end of the river and many boats locking through but all is leisurely and relaxed. The river is quite shallow in places but is said to have a minimum depth of 3m. The banks are lined with reeds or trees and there is no sign of commercial shipping or industry. We go as far as Pahlen and in a quiet spot at the side of the river anchor fore and aft with a rope tied to a tree. Cuckoos' calls fill the air and at dusk a lone cow comes down to the water to drink. Pahlen is just a little rural town with a road and a river running through. We take the dinghy ashore next morning but when we return we find the level of the river has gone down and we are just touching bottom - a few nasty moments until we pull ourselves free and then we are off down river to another delightful anchorage.

*The Eider River - waiting to enter the Lexfähre Lock*

The Eider River
The Kiel Canal
Brunsbüttel

21

## Eider River to Rendsburg

54°18'.50N / 09°40'.00E  – 25NM

## *Monday 1st June*

We return to the Lexfähre lock in late afternoon. The whole process of locking through is very time-consuming - at each lock someone from each boat has to scramble ashore and go into the lock-keeper's office to pay - your boat's name and its length are written down laboriously. Continuing along the Kiel Canal we come to Rendsburg tucked away in its own little waterway and make our way into a bight on the west side - it is calm and sheltered and we manage to moor up in a box without damage to boat or nerves.

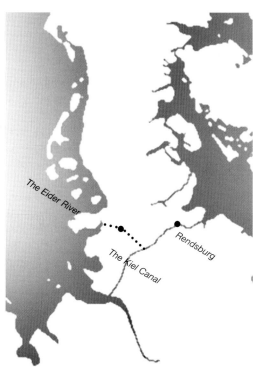

*Transporter Bridge across the Kiel Canal, near Rendsburg*

**Rendsburg**

*Tuesday 2nd June*

**CRUISING INFORMATION REPORT**

*RENDSBURG*

*A number of small marinas, some private but which welcome visitors. Mooring almost entirely box system. Water and electricity available.*

We are at the Eider Marina Rendsburg - a grand name for a tiny sailing club! It is very well kept - stern posts and bows-to staging - water and electricity - a small area of grass and flowers and all surrounded by trees and little houses. Through a gap in the trees we can see the frequent trains - it reminds us of Docklands - but here the trains are mostly goods - how do they manage to persuade businesses to keep things off the road? We walk round to the boat-yard at the head of the bight. The elderly proprietor speaks good English and will be very happy to take us for the winter - he shows us round the facilities - all seems satisfactory and so we arrange to come back some time in September, telephoning a few days ahead. The owner of the boat next to us is also very friendly and confirms this is a good place to overwinter - he says there are several other boatyards in the near vicinity if for any reason space is not available here - and he offers to keep an eye on our boat whilst we are back in England.

It is a bright sunny and warm day. Strolling into town for the inevitable shopping, it seems that few shops take credit cards - we buy video films from one who does but his system fails so we have to part with our cash again! During the afternoon several hours are spent scrubbing the pine needles and grime from our decks and trying to remove some of the brown staining which accumulated on the hull whilst in the various canals.

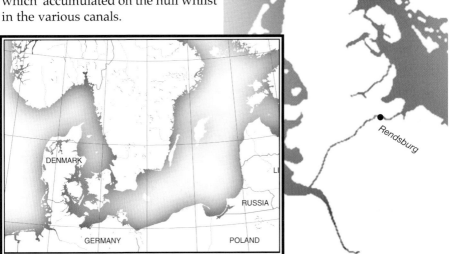

DENMARK

LI

RUSSIA

GERMANY          POLAND

Rendsburg

### Rendsburg to Holtenau

54°22'.17N / 10°08'.73E – 18NM

## *Wednesday 3rd June*

We put into Flemhude See for lunch; here you are permitted to anchor for one night in an area bordered by yellow buoys - a very pretty lake with reeded and tree-lined banks. We continue on our way to Holtenau and lock through - at last we have arrived in the Baltic. We tie up at the high staging just outside the locks - it is quite a scramble to get ashore. Having a need to visit the chart agent at the other side of the locks - we have to walk back down the road, take the free ferry across the canal and then walk back to the chart agent's office. This is in a customs area and we have to obtain a form to enter! However, the effort is well rewarded - we are able to purchase one of the Russian charts of Moon Sound (Estonia).

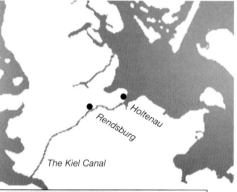

The Kiel Canal

*Passing ship in the Kiel Canal*

24

## Holtenau to Rødby Havn (Denmark)

54°39'.42N / 11°20'.98E – 48NM

*Thursday 4th June*

CRUISING INFORMATION REPORT

*RØDBY HAVN*

*Yachts moor in former commercial dock with basic but adequate facilities. Tie alongside quay walls.*

The wind is SW/W F2-4 and we are able to sail all day with main and poled-out genoa - sometimes the genniker - with frequent changes of sail and sail configurations. At times black clouds form around us but we have only a few spots of rain. We had hoped to reach Gedser but in the event the wind dies away and we put into Rødby Havn. Here yachts tie up to concrete walls in the old docks - the facilities are adequate and there is plenty of space.

We have no Danish money so our first call is to the bank, followed by a quick trip into a supermarket. Rødby is only a small town - one long street, few shops and many of the buildings are painted the traditional yellow ochre or vermilion. The Harbour Master's office is closed - hours are 0800 to 1700.

*The Holtenau Locks at the Baltic end of the Kiel Canal*

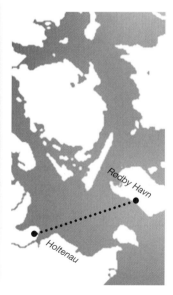

# Rødby Havn to Stubbekøbing

54°53'.49N / 12°02'.73E – 58NM

## Friday 5th June

**CRUISING INFORMATION REPORT**

*STUBBEKØBING*

The yacht harbour is very shallow as is the approach channel. It is possible to moor in the adjacent commercial harbour but facilities are only "basic".

Departure 0700 on a day of excellent visibility and almost clear blue sky. There is a NW F2 and a calm sea, under spinnaker we are making 5kts. We sail along the coast of the island of Lolland - across the water to the south we can see the German coast - lines of wind generators, a few tall buildings and a tall plume of smoke perhaps from Rostock, 25 miles away. Needing a Gaz refill and detailed local chart we put into Gedser but all is closed for yet another public holiday so we decide to press on to Stubbekøbing. A fortunate shift in the wind - we now have a SE F2-3 - gives us a pleasant sail up the wooded coast of the island of Falster until we see the buoys leading to Grønsund. Without a detailed chart we find it difficult to make the yacht harbour - the depth drops to 2m in the approach channel - we therefore put into the commercial harbour - again it is a concrete wall with rubber tyres!

Next day we obtain a Gaz refill (horrific price) and a local chart but now await a favourable wind. In Denmark the shops close Saturday p.m. and all day Sunday but not so Stubbekøbing's famous motor cycle museum (Europe's largest). This is fascinating - many very old bikes and names which bring back long forgotten memories, plus a collection of radios and early gramophones. As evening comes on a fog rolls in until we can hardly see the top of the silo which dominates the harbour. A boat comes alongside, the crew say they found it terrible outside.

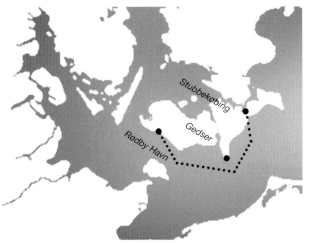

## Stubbekøbing to Klintholm Havn

54°57'.20N / 12°28'.00E  – 26NM

## Sunday 7th June

**CRUISING INFORMATION REPORT**

*KLINTHOLM HAVN*

New modern yacht harbour adjacent old fishing harbour (visiting yachts no longer permitted to use the latter). Berthing alongside or in boxes. Electricity and water. Bank, hotel and general store.

The fog has cleared and the wind has dropped. We cast off and immediately find the autopilot, which has given a few problems recently, has finally died on us. There is little to be done about it until we reach our next port which we decide will be Klintholm. Two long and two short tacks bring us to the harbour where we find a new modern marina village has been built beside the old fishing harbour - where only local yachts are now permitted. The marina itself is very pleasant with all facilities but very expensive - south of England prices. The village consists of a røgere (for smoking fish), one tiny bank, one hotel and a Spar grocer. All our attempts to revive the autopilot fail. The little marina quickly fills with visiting boats and we are pleased to see SNOWBIRD - whom we met in Helgoland. Klintholm is on the island of Mons which is famous for "Mons Klint" - Denmark's only high chalk cliffs. The pilot book says it is a 3 mile walk to the cliffs but we estimate it is 5 - and it is now a hot sunny afternoon. From the cliff top strong wooden steps descend to the beach. A German coming up tells us there are 470 steps - later the Harbour Master says 500, we can believe them. From the chalk beach the cliffs rise straight up - notices warn of frequent cliff falls. In a flat country anything high would be spectacular but these cliffs are quite awe-inspiring.

*The skipper and the chalk cliffs of Mons Klint*

*Denmark - the great chalk cliffs of Mons Klint*

27

### Klintholm Havn to Køge

55°28'.19N / 12°11'.84E – 45NM

## *Monday 8th June*

The forecast is for SSW Force 5-6, other boats are leaving for Sweden but we must go to Køge where the nearest Autohelm agent is located. We pass the massive cliffs and have a pleasant sail towards Stevn Klint on Sjælland where there are more but smaller chalk cliffs. The wind rises steadily from around F3 to 5 gusting 6 and, as we turn into Køge Bight, we are beating into the wind and thankful to enter harbour. The entrance is quite shallow but the sea is calm and we are relieved to find alongside staging. The Autohelm agent is right here in the marina and thinks he can solve the problem. The waterfront is spoilt by industrial plant with tall smoking chimneys and the air filled with a strong smell from the rubber and chemical works and wood processing plant.

**CRUISING INFORMATION REPORT**

**KØGE**

*Shallow in harbour entrance but plenty of depth within. Yacht harbour consists of several long fixed pontoons. Visitors can lie alongside hammerheads. Electricity and water available. The town is about a mile away but has all shops, banks, restaurants etc. Small shop and chandlers also Autohelm agent in harbour complex*

*Køge - Church where a fire was lit high up on the tower as a guiding light for seamen*

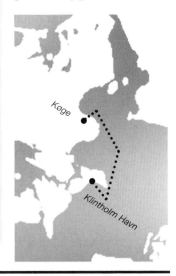

# Køge

## Tuesday 9th to Wednesday 10th June

The autopilot is fixed and reinstalled during Tuesday morning - but needs final calibration. The old medieval town lies behind the industrial waterfront and is very well preserved. The buildings centre around the large market square from the corners of which roads lined with quaint old houses lead away. The buildings are mostly brightly painted-yellow ochre and vermilion

Køge – the market square

and sometimes a less familiar blue. A local seeing us with cameras welcomes us to the town and tells us about the church - Sanct Nicholai Kirke and points out the "fireplace" high up in the tower where a fire was lit in olden times to act as a beacon for sailors. In nearby Kirkstraese (Church Street) No. 20 is one of Denmark's oldest houses -above the door is carved the date 1527.

Køge - No 20 Church Street, one of Denmark's oldest houses

# DENMARK TO SWEDEN

**Køge to Ystad**

55°25'.59N / 13°48'.88E  – 61NM

## *Thursday 11th June*

There is little wind and the visibility is mediocre. Nevertheless we are able to see the coast of the Falsterbo peninsular several miles off. All light weather sails get an airing today - some don't work for very long! Ystad is a large commercial and ferry port - yachts and fishing boats have a separate harbour with entrance to the west. There is plenty of space - visitors mostly tie up to one long pontoon. The town is large and attractive with many very old buildings painted in the same yellow ochre and vermilion as in Denmark. Konsum, the supermarket, is still open and offers the opportunity to buy some delicious Swedish ice cream; generally the food looks very good.

**CRUISING INFORMATION REPORT**

*YSTAD*

Yacht and fishing harbour located west of commercial harbour with separate entrance. Visitors moor to long pontoon, some boxes also available. Electricity and water on pontoon. Chandlers nearby.

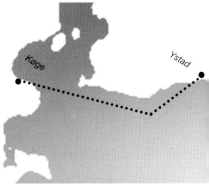

*Køge, the attractive and colourful old buildings*

## Ystad to Allinge (Bornholm)

55°16′.71N / 14°48′.12E – 37NM

*Friday 12th June*

In Ystad we meet a German couple in an X-boat - Schnubbel. They are going to Allinge on the Danish Island of Bornholm, we decide to do likewise. There is enough wind to sail slowly but the wind picks up once we have rounded the northern tip of the island and we have a good but short sail down the east coast to Allinge. Allinge harbour is old and tiny, a former fishing harbour and well protected. In really bad weather the gates to the inner harbour are closed. Yachts tie up around the perimeter - it is already full so we tie up alongside Schnubbel. Ashore there is a great deal of understandable noise and excitement some of which continues to the early hours; Denmark has just beaten Saudi Arabia in the World Cup!

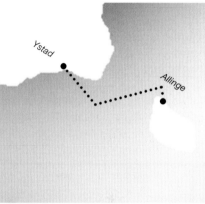

*The Falsterbo Light which stands in the middle of a "roundabout" at the junction of three shipping lanes*

## Saturday 13th June

It is a beautiful day with sunshine and excellent visibility but also blowing a strong westerly - around a F6 but we need no excuse to stay. Bornholm is a beautiful island very much favoured by German and Scandinavian holidaymakers. We take a bus ride round the island stopping at various other tiny and attractive harbours mostly along the east coast. At Rønne, the main port, we have to change buses to travel to the top of the island where we leave the bus to explore the Hammerhus castle ruins - despite massive maintenance works there is no charge to visit the site. The castle sits high on a rocky hilltop - a marvellous look out and reasonably easily defended. We walk back to Allinge by way of Sandvig - another tiny port and join Günter and Eleonore (SCHNUBBEL) for a drink in the evening.

Ronne Harbour, Bornholm

Allinge, Bornholm

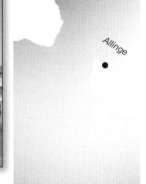

## Allinge to Utklippan (Sweden)

55°57'.24N/15°44'.21E – 51NM

## Sunday 14th June

Another day of beautiful unbroken sunshine and a gentle E wind - ideal for the genniker. Away to starboard we can see the tiny islets of Christiansø and Fredericsø which we visited in 1995. At length Bornholm disappears behind us but it is not lonely out here - there is a tremendous amount of shipping - all types and nationalities - including the inevitable rusty Russian carrying a deck cargo of wood. SCHNUBBEL is not far behind and other yachts are sighted from time to time. Depths sometimes exceed 90 m - we are now in the Baltic 'proper' and heading for Utklippan, a tiny and wild island, little more than a collection of rocks connected by concrete quays, all for the purpose of maintaining

a lighthouse off the south eastern tip of the mainland at the entrance to Kalmar Sound. Entry can be made from either east or west, the entrances being offset with the 'harbour' between. No one now lives here except the lighthouse keeper, he collects the harbour dues, sells postcards and smoked fish.

> **CRUISING INFORMATION REPORT**
>
> **UTKLIPPAN**
>
> Yachts tie up to concrete quays. Basic facilities consist of one electric point on one quay only, no water at all. Toilet. Lighthouse keeper is HM and collects dues, also sells smoked fish and postcards.

*Utklippan - approaching the lighthouse on a calm evening*

It is an ideal evening for a barbecue - we share resources with Günter and Eleonore. The gulls are quite ferocious - their young still cannot fly and are helpless, but one bold adult tries to steal food from our barbecue right beside us.

## Utklippan

### *Monday 15th to Wednesday 17th June*

The promised gale does not materialise on Sunday night but morning brings heavy and continuous rain - the first serious rain we have experienced for some time. The wind, although not strong, has now become northerly. The only boat to move is a motor boat going south - for the remaining seven boats - we stay quietly in our cabins (we are four Swedes, two Germans and one Brit). During Monday night the wind rises and becomes westerly - a scend comes into the harbour setting the boats jerking and running back and forth along the quayside. We are all tied on with several spare lines but every so often there is a bang as a warp breaks. We are even driven to put rubber tyres on the side of the boat - better black marks than the effect of a concrete wall. This ferocious wind -

*Utklippan - south westerly gale*

never less than a F7 and often as high as F9 - continues during Tuesday and Wednesday (and does not abate in fact until Thursday midday). No one expected the wind to last for so long. What is more, in *"The Baltic Sea"* - the most comprehensive pilot book - Barry Sheffield describes this harbour as having complete shelter. For much of the time

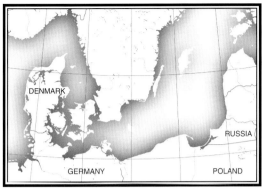

there is rain - in the dry periods figures clad in wellies and souwesters appear for a brief few minutes - it is the spirit of camaraderie that keeps us all going. On Tuesday the Harbour Master leaves for Karlskrona - he has a powerful engine and presumably is confident about the way out - he does not return until Thursday. On Wednesday a coastguard plane is seen flying low overhead - presumably to see we are all still alive. By this time food is beginning to run low on some boats and there is talk of a seagull hunting party. We all suffer a thoroughly miserable and stressful time - there is dark talk of selling boats or returning home. We can have little sleep - the motion of the boats and constant jerking is too uncomfortable - and the risk of damage and the need to be ready to leap out an ever constant stress.

*Utklippan - the boats attempting to survive the gale*

# Utklippan to Sandhamn

56°05'.57N / 15°51'.48E – 11NM

## Thursday 18th June

At first the wind is still F8 and the sea still pounding over the wall but the wind begins to drop and everyone talks of escaping from this prison. The Harbour Master returns with his family and dog, the wind drops to a SW F6 and one by one we struggle to untie our welded on and broken lines and make our way out. We know that the greatest danger is getting out through the rocks and away from the island - after that with the wind astern it is a quick run up the coast under foresail alone. We and the two German boats head for Sandhamn which is peaceful and quiet. The sun is shining and we are able to get ashore and walk to the nearest little shop for fresh supplies and ice cream.

**CRUISING INFORMATION REPORT**

*SANDHAMN*

Visiting yachts tie alongside quays or to small pontoon.Water and electricity available. Small general store within walking distance. NB There are many Sandhamns in Sweden. This harbour is on the mainland at the entrance to Kalmarsund and should not be confused with the Sandhamn in the Stockholm Archipelago (which is sometimes referred to as the Cowes of Sweden).

*Kalmar narrows with Øland Road Bridge in the distance*

## Sandhamn to Kalmar

56°39'.60N / 16°21'.88E – 43NM

*Friday 19th June*

```
CRUISING INFORMATION
REPORT

KALMAR

In main yacht basin berthing is
mostly by stern buoys with limited
alongside spaces In other basins
yachts can berth alongside. Water
and limited number of electric
points. Showers, toilets, laundry in
harbour buildings. Diesel from fuel
berth. Chandlers, supermarkets,
banks etc. all nearby.
```

As a result of the big blow in Utklippan, some nylon line - suspected of being part of the short wave aerial suspension - is flying in the wind at the top of the mast. This could become entangled with the anemometer destroying the rotating plastic cups leaving us with no means of measuring wind speed. Thus the first thing we have to do is to haul the skipper up the mast (fourth time this trip) -fortunately Günter comes along at the right moment to help with the winching. Whilst at the top of the mast, it is discovered that the Vitronix VHF antenna has been stripped of its GRP outer coating leaving only the braid supported on the inner core with the red top cap still in place. We have found some difficulty with radio communication recently and maybe this is the cause. The aerial will need replacing but this will not be possible until next year.

Whilst in Utklippan we also noticed that the LCD display on the Nasa Navtex marine information receiver on which we obtain weather forecasts etc in English has started to break down making it impossible to read some of the words. This receiver is the best we have being very sensitive. It picks up the signals at a better range than the ICS receiver which we use as a back-up. The boat is now into its sixth season and it seems that equipment is breaking down fast. We leave without having time to clear all the mess but feel it best to continue on our way whilst we have a good SW wind. Today we have mostly full main and poled out genoa plus from time to time the genniker too. Although occasional clouds loom it is mostly a bright and sunny day with excellent visibility. Our way lies through Kalmarsund - the passage between the mainland and the island of Öland, at first wide but the channel narrows just before Kalmar, there seems only just room for us to squeeze between the lighthouse and the buoys - all marking rocks. We have visited Kalmar previously and again tie up to the wall just before the main harbour basin.

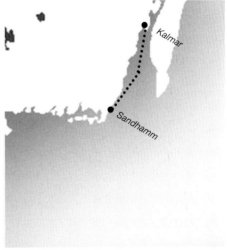

## Kalmar

*Saturday 20th to*
*Sunday 21st June*

It is midsummer - a festival celebrated with great gusto in Scandinavian countries - but this means another excuse to have a public holiday - in Kalmar not only is everything shut on Friday but also on Saturday - the food shops open for a brief time on Sunday but the chandlers is shut for the whole time. The Swedes are as ever outnumbered - there are many German boats, some Danes, Finns, Poles, Dutch, one French, one Austrian and us - a Czech boat is spotted in another harbour. On Sunday we discover another Red Ensign - fellow CA members Chris and Cecily in "KAOS II" from Largs on the west coast of Scotland. They are hoping

*Kalmar - the castle*

*Kalmar - anchor with view of the castle*

to reach Helsinki via Estonia so we swop information. The weather is hot and sunny and Kalmar has much of interest. Dominating all the Slott (castle) on its mound with surrounding moat. The Slott is a favourite place for weddings - we see two on our visit. The original town was sited near the castle but its wooden houses were mostly destroyed in a disastrous fire in the mid 17th century. The King of that time gave permission for the town to be rebuilt in its present setting across the river but only on condition that the houses were built of stone. Behind the grid pattern town there are tiny lakes where local boats are kept and people fish. We cycle out to see the bridge linking Öland with the mainland. At 6.072 km this is said to be the longest bridge in Europe - it is now receiving maintenance and there is scaffolding on one of the columns.

As we approach the bridge we find a red double decker bus in a layby - and a notice that cycling is not allowed on the bridge between the hours of 0700 and 1900. We discover that this free bus is provided to take bikes and riders across the bridge. As Sweden presumably has no doubledeckers, they have purchased a secondhand bus from Blackpool and converted the lower deck to accommodate cycles (they hang on hooks from the ceiling and are secured by chains like prisoners). Passengers travel on the upper deck. The bus still has all the signs from its days in Blackpool - pay your fare or else, etc! We speedily avail ourselves of this service - riding across the bridge on the top deck of a bus has to be preferable to cycling the 6+km!

Whilst in Kalmar, we also take the opportunity to catch up on cleaning the boat and dealing with the laundry. From the Harbour Office we obtain a copy of the latest version of '*Bätturist*' - the free harbour guide produced by the Tourist Authority. This is now much reduced in size - only Sweden is included. Our 1995 version, which we luckily have on board, also covered the other Scandinavian countries. We are relieved however to read in the new edition

that the former military areas prohibited to 'foreigners' are no longer restricted in peacetime - this is good news as we wish to visit Fårösund which was formerly in a forbidden area. We are experiencing difficulties in obtaining English- language weather forecasts but manage to pick up some from Stockholm Radio. Here wind speed is measured in metres per second - (quick rule-of-thumb conversion: divide by 2 = Beaufort).

## Kalmar to Borgholm (Öland)

56°52′.90N / 16°39′.00E  – 24NM

*Monday 22nd June*

The chandler opens at last - there is a queue outside by 0900. We purchase Swedish pilot books, new warps and one of the hooks used by Swedes to attach the stern of the boat to buoys - the favourite system of mooring  here is stern to buoy and  bows to quay. Before leaving harbour we take

**CRUISING INFORMATION REPORT**

*BORGHOLM (ÖLAND)*

*Modern yacht harbour with ample space for visitors. Mooring is stern buoy, bows to pontoon. Water and electricity on pontoon.Showers, toilets, cafe at harbour office.Small town closeby with all facilities, shops, banks, restaurants etc.*

the opportunity to fill with diesel and then we are back in the Sound and following the narrow channel under  the road bridge and  northwards. The wind is north easterly 2-3 and we make good progress tacking. The air is so clear that we can see the land on either side and ships right up  to the horizon. The only things that are difficult to see are the buoys marking the starboard side of the channel - they are thin  emaciated things - as are all the buoys in this part of the world. When they are sighted they have a strong resemblance to painted withies. We arrive in the very comfortable marina at Borgholm in mid afternoon - by now the sky has clouded over and threatens rain.

*Kalmar - Tam o'Shanter dressed overall for Midsummer*

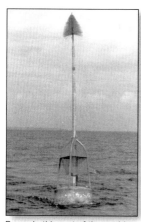

*Buoys in this part of the world are often thin, emaciated things*

## Borgholm to Byxelkrok

57°19'.67N / 17°00'.32E – 33 NM

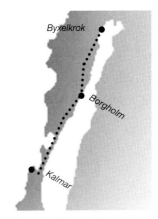

### Tuesday 23rd June

As we arise the rain starts to fall - just a gentle rain with little wind. We say farewell to Günter and Eleonore - who think it will be warmer in Denmark. We manage to sail for a time in a light north westerly but the wind drops away picking up again as an even lighter northeast-north. It is a thoroughly wet and miserable day - gone is the attractive blue and green vista of sea and shore lined with pinkish boulders - now all is in different shades of grey - even the beautiful island of Blä Jungfrun at the entrance to Kalmar Sound is grey. Several yachts leave Borgholm but the others are making for the mainland. After what seems a slow and tedious journey we arrive in Byxelkrok by late afternoon and try out our new stern mooring hook which works very successfully. Ashore there is little except a small supermarket (where we buy ice cream and fish), a few houses and fishermen's huts. A Swede on the next boat tells us that the German weather bureau has promised two months of summer starting tomorrow.

### CRUISING INFORMATION REPORT

#### BYXELKROK

*Small harbour with limited space for visitors - moor either alongside wall just inside harbour or using stern buoy to one of the pontoons. Electricity and water available. General store nearby.*

*Sailing north from Kalmar - the Öland Bridge*

### Byxelkrok to Visby (Gotland)

57°38′.29N / 18°17′.23E  – 50NM

## *Wednesday 24th June*

**CRUISING INFORMATION REPORT**

*VISBY*

*Capital of Gotland and a ferry port. Yacht harbour is crowded in the height of summer but it may be possible to arrange space in the adjoining basin. Mooring mostly by stern buoy, bows to pontoon. Water and electricity available. Showers, toilets, laundry, washing up facilities at harbour office. Excellent shopping facilities in town, banks, restaurants, car and cycle hire etc.*

By morning the wind is not too strong  but it is still dull and drizzling. We change our foresail for the working jib and cast off. One tack to take us away from the island and offlying rocks then we can make the course for Visby. The wind is slightly E of N F4-5 at first later F3-4 but the sea is lumpy.  During  the day the wind backs slightly to W of N and we have a really good sail. As we approach Gotland the wind inevitably dies away and headsails are changed and the genniker hoisted. The water is very deep - the maximum recorded during the day is 120 m and even close to the shore of Gotland we still find 80 m. Visby is a ferry port and, needless to say, a ferry is leaving just as we arrive!  The sun has at last broken through and we arrive to a sunny and summery harbour. We see KAOS II across the pontoon and on the wall beside the  harbour office is a boat from Lithuania but most visitors are Finnish.

*Gotland - Sheep in the streets of Visby*

# Visby

## Thursday 25th June

At the top of the hill it is a beautiful sunny day but at sea level a thick seamist rolls in obscuring the harbour. Visby is an old Hanseatic town, enclosed by walls which are still kept in good repair. The town is built on a steep hill, quaint twisting cobbled streets with houses all piled on top of one another. There are 11 churches all in ruins but the spires of the cathedral, which is in good condition, dominate the skyline. The Gotland emblem is a sheep - in Visby life-sized effigies are used to stop cars entering the pedestrian areas.

Visby Street scene

# SWEDEN TO THE BALTIC STATES

## Visby to Fårösund

57°51'.85N / 19°03'.64E  – 41 NM

## *Friday 26th June*

A bright and sunny start although the air seems always cold. We leave around
0900 in a SW F4 and have a pleasant sail along the west side of Gotland. The
island is heavily wooded, the shoreline low cliffs. Occasionally there is a green
patch where trees have been cleared and a few little houses or fishermen's huts
built. There are low cliffs north of Visby but as we turn towards Fårösund the
cliffs give way to sandy beaches. This used to be a military restricted area - the

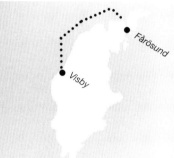

*Visby Harbiour*

military are still here and the sound of rapid gunfire greets us at the entrance to the Sound (the waterway between the islands of Gotland and Fårö). The water around is still very deep - we again record depths over 100m at sea but in the Sound there is only a narrow channel with sufficient water for shipping. The wind drops away from time to time - the spinnaker is hoisted but hastily dropped when a temporary wind shift wraps it around the forestay. At the point where the ferry crosses between the islands there is a small settlement with two little harbours - we pick

**CRUISING INFORMATION REPORT**

*FÅRÖSUND*

*Small yacht harbour east of ferry crossing. Has corps mort system but when not overcrowded yachts can lie alongside wooden staging. Electricity on pontoon. Water and diesel on quay near harbour office. Toilets, showers, chandlery at harbour office.*

Mercuria the smallest but with no fishing or commercial craft where boats can tie up alongside staging. KAOS II arrives a little later and ties up behind us. Our first task is an engine oil change and some boat cleaning. Our ensign is now faded and becoming too frayed - before we arrive in the Baltic States we change it for something newer. We spend the evening helping Chris and crew reduce their drink store and in discussion discover that Chris and I once went to the same school in Ashtead!

*In 1998 we sailed overnight from Fårösund to Ventspils, Latvia and, thence, to Nasva, Estonia. So that we may include more information on Baltic States harbours, we have here included extracts from our 1999 and 2000 cruise logs.*

*Gotland - Swedish Milestone (1 Swedish Mil =10 km)*

*Gotland - coastal stacks*

### Fårösund to Liepaja (Latvia)

56°30'.76N / 21°00'.80E  – 114NM

## Wednesday 2nd June 1999

At 4a.m. the sun is up, the wind is south westerly and we are on passage to Liepaja. The wind holds up enabling us to sail all the way and at an average speed of 6.4 kts. Although the air is cold, the sun shines all day with never a cloud to be seen. There is some commercial shipping hurrying south - the two passing closest are Russians with deck cargoes of wood but all day we see only one yacht. The Latvian coast is low-lying and cannot be seen until we are about 10 miles off. We make the harbour entrance just as the sun is setting and call Port Control. In excellent English we are told to proceed to the yacht moorings - up river just below the bridge - and "an agent will be telephoned". On the way up river everything we see tells a story of neglect - tumbledown buildings and rusting ships. A reception committee is awaiting us - the agent and at least three  smartly uniformed Border Guards plus a few other bodies, one of whom seems to mastermind the exercise.  The only one to come aboard is the agent - a pleasant young man with reasonable English. Passports are examined in great detail, crew lists stamped and then they all go away.  We are tired so just fall into bed at 23.30.  [Latvia in 1999 was one hour ahead on Eastern European Time (UTC +3) but in 2000 had changed to Central European time (UTC + 2)].  It is peaceful enough here and very sheltered - the only disturbance being the sound of trams crossing the bridge.

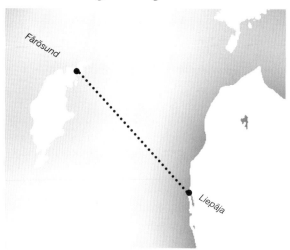

> **CRUISING INFORMATION REPORT**
>
> *LIEPAJA*
> *(pronounced Leea pie ya)*
>
> The approaches to Liepaja harbour are shallow and in bad weather conditions can be regarded as unsafe. Of the three entrances only the southern and central openings can be considered as safe. Yachts are expected to use the southern entrance. The outer harbour, enclosed by  breakwaters, has numerous wrecks and is also very shallow (particularly at the southern end). It is imperative to follow the leading marks and buoys. The yacht moorings lie some distance up river on the starboard side just below the bridge and are well sheltered under normal weather conditions. Berthing is alongside staging, rafting out when necessary. Water and electricity beside berths. Toilets and showers in facilities building beside the quay.  Fuel berth down river or diesel can be brought in cans from nearby fuel station. Post office, banks, restaurants, supermarket, markets are all conveniently located in nearby streets.

**Liepaja**

## Thursday 3rd /Friday 4th June 1999

Little more than 100 miles away we left the sophisticated, well to do, comfortable west - this town is a culture shock. Once a favourite holiday resort of the aristocracy in Tsarist Russian times it is now a scene of neglected former splendour. The once elegant villas are still standing (just) but badly in need of paint and repair, everywhere it is the same picture, although some roads are being repaired. It is hot and dust lies everywhere, even the dandelions look depressed. The open air fruit and vegetable market is bright and lively, the produce looks fresh and colourful. There is too an indoor market with meat and fish - no shortages of food here. Both the Evangelical Church and the Catholic Cathedral are quite ornate and in reasonable repair. The "residential" area has unmade roads lined with trees and grass verges - here and there a modern bungalow stands out, surrounded by a tended garden and smart painted fence. All across town on most street corners there are water pumps all in working order. At a filling station near to the quay we buy diesel in cans at the cost of .27 Lats/lr (30p/lr) but when we return to the quay we find everyone else has bought diesel delivered by the Russians at .16 Lats/lr!

We walk to a Russian church some distance away on the other side of the river. On the way we pass huge empty factories, under the Soviet system goods were mass produced in some region for the whole Soviet empire - Liepaja manufactured ladies, underwear. The church was originally set in graceful parkland with wide straight tree-lined roads and the villas of the Russian aristocracy - some of these now used as army barracks - now it is surrounded by the ugliest monstrosities, concrete blocks of flats in appalling states of disrepair. We catch a bus back, buy tickets from the driver - 12 cents each (14p) - and sit down. Next thing a Kleb-like character but not in uniform is asking for something (my first thought is she is a beggar) - we produce the tickets thinking they have to be shown - but, no, we seem to have contravened some rule and are to be fined 1 Lat (£1.13). We protest we have paid for the tickets. So what is wrong. The woman speaks no English so the skipper, after attempting to sort it out with the driver, jumps up and asks if anyone on the bus speaks English - someone explains we should have punched the tickets in the small machines provided. Another woman grabs the tickets, punches and gives them back - then they both get off the bus and we have narrowly avoided a fine!

## Liepaja to Klaipeda (Lithuania)

55°41'.80N / 21°07'.27E – 60NM

*Saturday 5th June 1999*

We check out of Latvia and set off for Lithuania in a light wind. We are called up by the Pape Light just after midday - what is the name of our vessel where have we come from and where do we go - all friendly but he has difficulty understanding our name - the skipper has to spell it out even slower "tango, alpha, mike ...", then our nationality - "British", "can you repeat" - "English" - that seems to satisfy him. Klaipeda lies on one side of a river which widens to become the Curonian Lagoon, the southern part of which is in Russia. On the town side the waterfront is lined with busy docks, on the other side is a narrow promontory of land with a splendid beach. A call to Port Control proves unproductive but we soon see a large notice pointing out the location of Customs and Immigration - a police launch comes out and beckons us to follow. The quay to which we are directed is absolutely awful - rough concrete with iron protruding and great black fenders - and not helped by the washes of passing ships and the ferry. When the officials arrive they have great difficulty getting aboard but make no complaint - one is a young girl very smartly attired (mini skirt, high heels and tights!). The skipper fills in forms whilst I fend off - everything here is geared to ships, what is your cargo?

*Liepaja - indoor market*

*Liepaja - yachts moor beneath the trees*

What stores do you carry? You can just put a line through whatever is not applicable! Communication is not easy - only the young girl has limited English (and the skipper's Lithuanian is not fluent!). Yachts berth at the Klaipeda Yacht Club, which lies on the opposite side of the river (a public ferry carries passengers back and forth to the town). The yacht club has two adjacent basins, the berths in the inner are too narrow and shallow for us but the outer basin has deeper water and berths designed for larger craft. We visit the Harbour Master's office to report in. He speaks no English but others help and later he comes round to make sure we are OK and to tell us about water, showers etc (in sign language and German!).

*Liepaja - street scene*

## Klaipeda

### Sunday 6th to Thursday 10th June 1999

In beautiful summer weather we take the ferry to town. It is very much a holiday atmosphere with many people coming across to visit the beach - little horse-drawn -taxis wait to drive folk away as well as conventional buses and taxis going down the peninsular to Nida. Across the river the ferry docks at Old Castle Port (apparently no longer available to visiting yachts). The ferry runs half hourly on the quarter to and past the hour from the yacht club side and on the hour and half past the hour from the town side the fare is 1.4 Litas per person paid only on the town side. All day we explore the town and realise that Lithuania has now progressed further than we had been told. Part of Klaipeda is modern with tree-lined streets, shops with

Klaipeda - buying small cucumbers in the outdoor market

Klaipeda - the Customs/Immigration quay

*Klaipeda, Old Castle Harbour - no longer in use for visiting yachts*

expensive goods, and areas of tree-shaded park, one with over 100 sculptures, and buildings in good repair. There is also the old town with German-style Fachwerk buildings, the now familiar open-air market where we buy bananas and tomatoes very cheaply, and indoor meat and fish markets. One of the club boats is sailing to England - and we give the skipper a printout of the Dover tidetable - he expects to go to Lowestoft and back in three weeks!

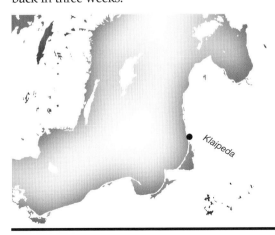

*Klaipeda, inner basin of the Klaipeda Sailing Centre - showing club premises*

We take the bus down to Nida, not far from the Russian border. Nida is a small holiday resort with a large harbour, quaint old fishermen's cottages, and an interesting amber museum.

When we return to Liepaja a few days later, we log a distance of 8NM less - there is a current running northwards caused by several days of southerly winds.

*Klaipeda - outdoor market - eggs go home in plastic bags*

# LATVIA

## Liepaja to Pavilosta

56°53'.31N/21°10'.51E – 30NM

*Saturday 12th June 1999*

The wind is E/NE 10 -11kts and we are soon speeding away northwards. There are still storms about but activity seems to stay over the land. It continues stiflingly hot and after a time the wind fails so we have to resort to engine for a while but manage the last few miles slowly under sail. Pavilosta is a very small port - no more than a narrow river entrance between two moles but all so very different from the towns. People wave to us as we enter and the Border Guards, who are expecting us, come out to say welcome - all they require is one crew

*Pavilosta harbour entrance*

list and this time they are more than pleased to take ours. We tie up to tall staging. Beside the quay is a smart new building - Club House, Harbour Master and Guards office plus showers and toilets. A young man from the Harbour Office strolls along the staging to have a chat and asks if there is anything we need or he can provide for us. His English is slow but he tells us he has spent some time studying in France, and thus the conversation continues in French. Ashore the road runs alongside the River Saka, the little village is charming, the houses in good repair, many wooden and colourfully painted. There are meadows full of wild flowers where the odd cow is tethered, people tending the crops, cottages in well kept gardens behind trimmed hedges, everywhere at this time of year the lilac is in great profusion. In the evening we buy a simple meal at the cafe, as always in Latvia the food is beautifully presented. A Russian lady who speaks some English helps by translating the menu and we meet up with her again later in the evening when we visit the beach and climb the look out tower. The shores of the eastern Baltic are lined with beautiful sandy beaches backed with sand dunes and pine forest.

**CRUISING INFORMATION REPORT**

*PAVILOSTA*

*Approach should be by daylight only. With onshore winds of F5 and over it is dangerous to enter and the harbour is "Closed". The quay is a short distance upriver and not directly open to the sea - it could likely suffer from swell in strong on-shore winds. Visitors' berths are alongside wooden staging on the port hand side adjacent the Yacht Club/HM/Border Guard Office. Water and electricity by arrangement - toilets and showers in YC building. One small general store and a couple of cafes where good food is available at reasonable prices.*

*Pavilosta - yachts tie up to wooden staging*

54

## Pavilosta to Ventspils

57°23'.62N / 21°13'.98E  –  37NM

### Sunday 13th June 1999

There are no formalities - so we leave - the wind enabling us to sail away from the staging. It is yet another scorching hot day, the wind mostly easterly off the land and itself hot, varying in direction and speed, from 7 to 20kts - the genniker is up and down, genoa out then reefed. Approaching Ventspils a call to Port Control proves unproductive. What is your ETA? Who is your agent? etc. As we approach the dreadful concrete quay where we cleared in and out last year we see two officers waving us on indicating that we should proceed to the yacht moorings in the fish dock - this is a relief. Yachts moor at one end

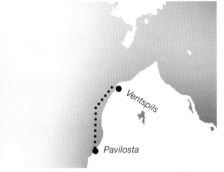

Pavilosta - Club House, Harbour and Border Guards office

of the fish dock where stern buoys have been laid and there is a good wooden staging with power supplies. The Harbour Master is waiting for us and takes our lines. He speaks no English so it is sign language and German - he doesn't want our forms but we have to fill in five giving exactly the same information – Border Guards are contacted by phone and are soon round – one speaks good English and is the usual cheerful young man as we have encountered here before. He tells us they have stopped using the awful quay and now come round to the yacht harbour to deal with formalities, saying "if it was my yacht I would not want to tie up to such a quay....". The harbour fee has almost doubled – from 4 Lats last year it is now 7.60 - about the pnces of Finland or Sweden but, as most of the visitors come from those countries and the facilities here are not too bad, can one blame the Latvians. We rest until the temperature cools down (max recorded temp during the day is 29.3°C) then have to do an oil change.

Ventspils - restored castle

## Ventspils

We have now made three visits to this town, each time staying a few days and seeing the friends made previously. On our first visit in 1998 we had sailed overnight from Fårösund (91 NM). Ventspils in 1998 was still emerging from the years of Soviet neglect – by 2000 much of the infrastructure work in the town has been completed – new mains and sewers laid and many roads and pavements block-paved. Ventspils has money from its oil terminal. The castle is being restored and the outdoor market has been rebuilt. From Ventspils we have taken bus trips to other towns, including Riga, Liepaja and Kuldiga. The bus provides an excellent opportunity to see the Latvian countryside – peaceful and rural – a mixture of forest and meadows, the roads lined with wild blue lupins and the chance to see nesting storks. The White Stork is common, building neat, basket-like nests, sometimes on chimneys, sometimes on telegraph poles, and adult birds can often be seen in the fields stalking frogs and other small creatures.

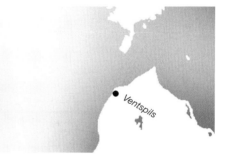

Ventspils - Yacht berths at the end of the Fish Dock

Kuldiga is a lovely old town on the banks of the river Venta (the same river which flows into the sea at Ventspils) with small streams flowing between the houses. Here the river is shallow with a natural weir, Europe's widest waterfall, children swimming and enjoying themselves. Most of the buildings, including several churches, are in reasonable state of repair.

*Kuldiga (Latvia) – River Venta*

*Ventspils, Open-air museum - this little train once ran on the line to Kurzeme*

## Ventspils to Roja

57°30'.38N / 22°48'.09E – 63NM

### Tuesday 30th May 2000

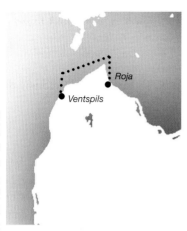

Roja

Ventspils

We leave at 0600 - the sky is full of grey clouds and there is a strong breeze but the wind will be behind us. We leave the harbour entrance under a sliver of foresail alone - outside the following sea is rolling but we have an excellent and fast passage keeping in sight of the shore - pinetree topped golden beach all the way. This is potentially one of the most difficult passages effectively being three sides of a square and we are lucky to have a wind which enables us to sail nearly all the way, it falls light then fails

about 6 miles off the entrance to Roja. By early afternoon we round Kolka point - from where a shallow spit runs out about 3 miles to a lighthouse - and turn southwards down the Gulf of Riga.

Roja fairway buoy is missing but there is a sector light to guide ships in. Roja now has a pontoon for yachts just below the road bridge in a sheltered river pool with grassy banks - very quiet and pleasant. As we are tying up two Border Guards arrive. Their English is limited, but they have a purpose-made phrase list - starting with "welcome to Roja" - but this does not help them understand our replies! Nevertheless the formalities do not take long and we are able to take a stroll ashore and enjoy a meal in the local hotel for less than £10. Roja has adequate shops, a bank and a few restaurants and the fisheries museum is worth visiting.

*Roja (Latvia) - new pontoon for yachts*

## Roja to Mersrags

57°20'.12N / 23,07'.68E – 20NM

## *Wednesday 31st May 2000*

The Harbour Master comes round for a chat in the early morning - there is no charge until facilities are installed. Fishermen are painting their boats - there is little fishing now they have lost their main market (Russia). We leave about midday to sail to Mersrags, first reporting out to the Border Guards. It is a day of sunshine but clouds are gathering and we can see storms over the shore. There is a gentle south westerly breeze off the land but every so often under the influence of the clouds the wind goes round in circles sending us fruitlessly tacking only to tack again in a few minutes. Some storms pass in front and others behind but as we approach Mersrags we run into a shower and storm - there is a sound of sparking behind me. The short-wave aerial is picking up a charge from the electrical storm and the sparking is the discharge across the lower insulator.

*Giant Abacus at Cesis (Latvia) - in the markets the abacus is still used to add up the bill but the result is shown to you on the display of a modern calculator!*

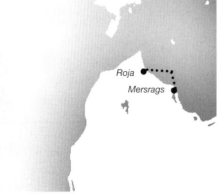

The White Stork nests on chimneys
and telegraph poles

The skipper hurriedly shorts the backstay to the water with a piece of chain and fortunately is not electrocuted in the process. All the aerials had in any case been disconnected, apart from the GPS -

Mersrags (Latvia) yachts moor to rusty pontoon just below the fishing boats

the next thing the GPS is down, the electrical storm has thrown it into total confusion. The Mersrags fairway buoy and channel buoys are all in place and there is a sector light here too. New quays have been built and piles of logs stand waiting for collection, but the port is quiet and there is no shipping only a couple of fishing boats being repaired. Yachts tie up to a rusty pontoon on the starboard side below the road bridge. The Harbour is open to the east and there is a slight swell coming in. This has obviously been a busy port in the past - there are many derelict and abandoned buildings. We are in a Customs Zone and the Border Guard eventually turns up, a woman bringing a boy of about 12 whose English she says needs improvement! More stamping of crew lists and we have to say when we will leave so she can come round again in the morning - the Guards office is on the opposite side of the harbour. There is no water or electricity available, nor toilets and showers. No one comes to visit us or charge us any money.

When the rain stops and some repairs have been carried out, the skipper decides to make a permanent earth for the backstay to avoid future problems with electrical storms, we take a walk ashore. We have good security in the Customs Zone with 24 hour guard on the gate, but we cannot see what they are guarding, there is little here but abandoned and wrecked buildings. Mersrags is a small sprawling village with a few shops and restaurants (Kafenicas). We see a sign to a place of interest at 3km - Engures Ezers the Engure Lake, a huge expanse of water and reedbeds running behind the coast from Engure to Mersrags. The track takes us through the forest, first passing by small houses in large plots of land, all very pleasant with well kept gardens. At the end of the track we find reed beds and a few men at some sheds working on small boats. Seeing our interest, the water can only just be seen above the reeds, one man takes us up the steps to a hide so we can get a better view and take photos.

*Engures Ezers - huge lake behind Mersrags*

57°09'.75N / 23°13'.93E  – 18NM

## Thursday 1st June 2000

The Border Guard arrives at 0830 - we expect to be away by 0900 so our crew list is stamped - next port of call  Engure.  Outside the wind is still in a muddle - it is light and 'variable' - it actually comes from every direction in turn and again we are tacking and retacking for nothing.  In the end we sail 18 miles for a 10-mile journey.  There are again heavy showers but no thunderstorms. As we approach Engure a Border Patrol boat passes closeby, the crew returning a friendly wave. Fishermen are landing nets off the entrance - the channel is narrow and very shallow - 3.2m the least depth.  There are leading marks for guidance, two striped boards to be kept in line.  The harbour is open to the east (it is said the prevailing wind is westerly) and guarded by moles - the extremities

**CRUISING INFORMATION REPORT**

*MERSRAGS*

*A commercial and fishing port with new commercial quays. From the fairway buoy sector light for approach - leading line 270T. Starboard and port hand buoys in entrance. Channel dredged recently - lowest depth on approach 6.7m. New moles have been constructed at harbour entrance. Open to the east in a very narrow sector - swell enters harbour.Would be uncomfortable in easterly winds. At present there is a rusty pontoon for yachts on the starboard side before the bridge. No water, electricity etc in 2000. General stores, cafes in small village nearby.*

*Mersrags - river bridge and water tower*

of which are merely wooden stakes. This is a different sort of harbour from Roja and Mersrags - the few fishermen work in small boats and there appears little commerce. There is a yacht club - a building of faded splendour on floats reached by a walkway and plank from the shore. There are local yachts and youngsters out sailing dinghies, mostly the ubiquitous Optimist. We tie up alongside the YC staging. Everyone is very friendly but shy to speak English. The harbour is shallow but very pretty with sand dunes surrounding. There are no Border Guards and no one charges us any money. Water and electricity are available and it appears showers and toilets may be available in season in little steep pitched thatched buildings. Beyond lies a small village with a few shops and restaurants. In the evening

we invite about 10 of the youngsters on board TAM O'SHANTER, they speak some English and ask lots of questions and give us a small pennant from their club - lovely kids.

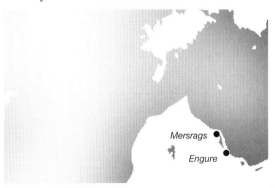

*Engure yacht club Pennant*

*Engure yacht club*

*Engure - general view of harbour*

### Engure to Riga

56°57'.56N / 24°05'.85E  – 39NM

## Friday 2nd June 2000

A peaceful night but the morning forecast is for a strong S/SW. In the event it is more S/SE about F4/5 but a cold and heavy wind. We have three reefs in the main and the foresail we reefed likewise and are going like a rocket at over 8kts. Although there is only a short fetch the sea in the Gulf of Riga produces a short sharp chop and can be unpleasant. The sky is overcast and there is some rain. It does not take long to reach the entrance to the River Daugava - we tack in and up river in true Arthur Ransome style. Riga lies 8 miles up-river - there is a strong current against us - the wind is on the nose for the last mile but

Riga - Arnis Berzins, Harbour Captain at Andrejosta Harbour (now the CA's HLR in Riga)

Riga - the Vansu Bridge

that is all we have to motor, by now it is pouring with rain. Just before Vansu Bridge we turn to port and enter Andrejosta yacht harbour where Arnis Berzins, the Harbour Master with whom we have corresponded during the winter comes out to welcome us and take our lines. There are 2 Finnish yachts here already but the Union Jack soon joins the Finnish flag over the yacht club. We recognise several local boats and note that there are now even more than on our previous visit.

Riga's oldest building - the Powder Tower

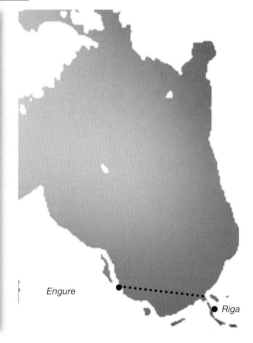

Engure

Riga

# Riga

Riga, capital of Latvia, has a compact old town situated not far from Andrejosta. We wander through the twisting streets of the medieval Hanseatic town and find so much of interest - the Swedish Gate, the 'Cat' House, the Powder Tower (Riga's oldest building), 'Milda' (freedom statue), and St

*Selling Amber - Folk Festival and Craft Fair at Jugla near Riga*

Peter's Church where one can take a lift to gain a magnificent view across the city, the newly restored House of the Blackheads and the poignant Museum of the Occupation. Not far from the old town are the markets, both indoor and outdoor and the bus and train stations. From these we travel cheaply all across

Latvia, visiting the towns of Cesis, Daugavpils, Sigulda, Jelgava, Jurmala (Jurmala is the collective name for a number of seaside holiday resorts), Jugla – a suburb of Riga where we spend two days at the Folk Festival and Craft Fair - and even as far afield as Vilnius, capital of Lithuania.

*Folk Festival at Jugla near Riga*

## Riga to Salacgriva

57°45'.46N / 24°42'.10E
– 55NM

*Tuesday 29th June 1999*

An early start - motoring down the river with no wind. Strange cloud formations make us a little apprehensive - but such forecasts as we have been able to obtain (the Navtex has not functioned in Riga) have suggested nothing untoward. After motoring for some time, a black cloud gathers behind us, the wind rises quickly to a F6 and down comes the rain - at least we can sail! But both the wind and rain are shortlived - the sun comes out and dries the decks and the wind fails. A couple of hours before we reach Salacgriva the wind rises again - we can hear thunder from a storm over the land - the sea rises and we are reefing but still flying along at over 7kts in a F5/6. With relief we sight the fairway buoy and run into the harbour. (In 1999

*Riga - the Swedish Gate*

Salacgriva had no proper facilities for yachts but in 2000 a pontoon had been provided). We tie up at an empty space on the quay between two commercial craft - one is unloading aggregate - there is dust and grit in great clouds but we are glad to be in harbour. The Border Guard is really friendly with good English - says he has never booked in a British yacht before. In a nearby restaurant we are presented with a small bottle of Rigas Balsam by the owner - a souvenir of Latvia. (Rigas Balsam is a herbal concoction – 45% proof – and a local speciality).

**CRUISING INFORMATION REPORT**

*SALACGRIVA (pronounced "Salasgreeva")*

A commercial port - entrance is well marked but rough in on shore winds. A pontoon for yachts has been installed just below the road bridge. A small village with a few shops and adequate cafes - good food at cheap prices.

Skulte, (Latvia) - small port not yet having designated place for yachts

# LATVIA TO ESTONIA

## Salacgriva to Pärnu

58°23'.20N/24°29'.35E – 48NM

## Wednesday 30th June 1999

The wind has abated sufficiently and we are soon stamped out of Latvia by another pleasant Guard. At the fairway buoy we raise sail and turn our course northwards towards Estonia. The sun is shining and we have a good wind - WSW F3/4 - so make a fast passage. Pärnu lies on

*Pärnu Yacht Club, Estonia*

the banks of a river in a bay at the north east corner of the Gulf of Riga. From the Pärnu fairway buoy we follow various sets of leading marks till we reach the yacht club tucked round the first bend and on the starboard side. The port hand bank is full of commercial docks - ships being loaded with logs but the yacht club side is pleasant and tree lined.

Parnu - Orthodox Church

The pontoons are packed - we just manage to squeeze in on the end of a pontoon (stern buoy - bows to quay). Customs and Immigration are telephoned and arrive speedily. The Customs Officer is so concerned about his bicycle (which he has left on the pontoon) that he just wants his form filled in asap - he does most of it himself. At the club we make contact with the CA's HLR (Honorary Local Representative) in Pärnu - Peeter Volkov - who comes aboard for a drink and a chat in the evening and gives us helpful information about sailing to the island of Kihnu - there are fishing nets to be avoided in places on the route.

Pärnu is a major holiday resort and known as Estonia's "Summer Capital". A popular resort with the Russian aristocracy, it still has elegant buildings from Tsarist times. The pleasant small town is a short walk from the yacht club as is the beautiful sandy beach. As we walk through the sand dunes towards the

## CRUISING INFORMATION REPORT

### PÄRNU

*A major commercial port with excellent facilities for yachts at the Parnu Sailing Club. Berthing by stern buoy or stern anchor to three pontoons. Water and electricity on pontoons. Showers and toilets in yacht club building. Diesel from fuel berth in harbour. Chandlers in yacht harbour. Excellent restaurant at the yacht club. The town of Parnu is a short walk from the harbour but has all facilities - shops, restaurants, banks, post office.*

beach, both of us are somewhat surprised to be stopped by a very young but friendly policeman from whom we learn that some areas of the beach are for ladies only – the skipper is permitted only on the "public" beach.

Yachts racing at Pämu – EST 245 is Peeter Volkov's Kexutaja

## Pärnu to Kihnu Island

58°08'.45N / 24°01'.05E  –  23NM

## Friday 2nd July 1999

We leave early, before the expected westerly wind has set in - in the event there is almost no wind and we have to motor on and off all the way. In the river entrance there are dredging operations - about which we have received a Navtex warning. The harbour at Kihnu is described - even by the Estonians - as in need of repair. This is no understatement though the first impression in bright sunshine is of a pretty little harbour with reeds to one side and a long pier to the south. The pier is used for the mainland ferry and has been repaired

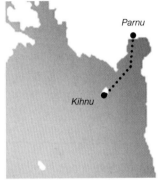

*Kihnu Island, Estonia - yachts tie alongside broken wooden posts*

- for the rest it is used by fishermen, and yachts tie to the remains of a log edging, mostly tipping over, behind which the ground has fallen away and is littered with rubbish, fishing crates and a few rocks.

Life cannot have changed here much in centuries, the roads are all unmade and full of dust - one has to leap into the bushes every time a car or tractor passes. A favourite means of transport is motorbike and side car - closer inspection shows these to be of Russian manufacture. The island supports a population of about 550 who live mostly by fishing and some tourism. Up to the time of the last war the population was Swedish and the houses are wooden, Swedish-style, often grouped together in farmsteads.

*From Kihnu Island we sailed to Virtsu, a distance of 42NM, firstly following buoyed channels between the low lying islands (where the buoys are so small as to be indistinguishable until you have nearly reached them - and some cardinal marks are missing) until we entered Moon Sound.*

*Kihnu Island, Estonia - typical homestead - motorbike and sidecar are favourite means of transport*

## Ventspils to Nasva (Estonia)

58°12'.98N / 22°23'.59E – 63NM

*Wednesday 1st July 1998*

We have to obtain a form from the Harbour Master to say we have paid all dues and hand this to the border control when we leave. We return to the concrete quay and formalities are quickly dealt with. Again we have to sign a paper that no stowaways were on board - we are told they have terrible problems with illegal immigrants from Turkey and Iraq. It is another misty morning but with adequate visibility and no wind. We motor off down the buoyed channel and along the coast to enter the Gulf of Riga by the Irbensky strait. There is some

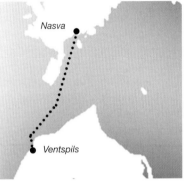

*Nasva Yacht Club, Estonia*

shipping about. At length the mist clears, the sun comes out and enough breeze picks up to enable us to sail. The coast of Estonia comes into view and we sail along the coast of the Island of Saaremaa until we pick up the fairway buoy leading to Nasva. In the entrance channel inside the harbour we run aground on a shallow patch but people call out to us the best route in and two lads in a dinghy lead us to the quay. They take our lines and go off to telephone Customs for us. Customs and Border Control (a lady) arrive soon afterwards and again the formalities are speedily dealt with - only two copies of the crew list are required this time.

The Union Jack is soon flying over the yacht club and at the office we enquire about charts - all information has led us to believe that, if we can get to Nasva, we can obtain charts here. It is a terrible shock to be told that they have few charts and no more can be obtained. We buy the most useful but are still left with little information on some parts of Estonia. Good navigation here is absolutely essential as the sea is strewn with boulders. The young man who took our lines works for the harbour office and he produces his Russian chart and arranges to copy the relevant parts the next day. We are left wondering whether we will be able to continue or have to abandon Tallinn and Helsinki and return to Sweden the way we have come. Nasva has little apart from the yacht club hotel but the area is green and pleasant and there are several yachts about - some local, some visiting Swedes.

*Windmills at Angla, Saaremaa, Estonia*

## Nasva

### Thursday 2nd July

We cycle to Kuressaare the capital of the island about 6 miles away. This is so different from Latvia - you could almost imagine yourself in an English market town - the buildings are in a reasonable state and painted in attractive colours - there is a tourist office where every-

*Kuressaare Castle, Saaremaa, Estonia*

one speaks excellent English and a banner across the street announces a performance of Shakespeare's *King John*. At the Tourist Office

ESTONIA

LATVIA

Nasva

### CRUISING INFORMATION REPORT

#### NASVA

*There are three harbours based on the town of Kuressaare - Nasva, Kuressaare and Roomassaare. In 2000 the entry channel leading to Nasva had shifted but the leading marks had not been moved to reflect this change thus boats ran aground whilst on the leading line. Nasva Harbour is under new management and it is intended to dredge to ensure the harbour can be approached safely. Kuressaare's new marina is currently (2000) unusable due to the existence of a rock and insufficient dredging of the approach channel.*

*Kuressaare, Saaremaa, Estonia -*
*the market lies behind these buildings*

they know there is a serious problem with the supply of sea charts and make enquiries for us as to what can be obtained - the answer is nothing on Saaremaa and it will take two days to obtain charts from Tallinn. We are able to buy a copy of the 1996 *Mini Loots* - the Estonian harbour guide (not as good as the 1994 version) and a chance meeting in the street with some Finns (who were also looking for *Mini Loots*) enables us to get copies of harbour diagrams from their Finnish guide. Perhaps we can survive after all. We enjoy an excellent and very cheap lunch, buy souvenirs and gifts in the market, and look at the castle.

**CRUISING INFORMATION REPORT**

*ROOMASSAARE*

*Roomassaare has a small modern marina situated 4 km east of Kuressaare. From the fairway buoy the approach is straightforward with leading marks and port and starboard hand buoys - albeit the buoys are small. Yachts berth alongside good individual finger pontoons. Water and electricity on pontoon. Toilets, showers and sauna in Harbour building. Diesel from fuel berth in harbour. Buses to Kuressaare from outside the marina. Small bar and restaurant at Clubhouse. All facilities in Kuressaare - shops, banks, post office, restaurants, car hire, good Tourist Office and an outdoor market.*

We also cycle on to Roomassaare where we find a new harbour with good shelter and finger berths. In the evening we eat at the Nasva Yacht Club - which also runs the hotel. The cuisine and menu are worthy of the best hotels anywhere. In the restaurant we meet with a Dane and his Estonian girlfriend - people using English as a common language. When we return to the boat the two boys, Preet and Toniel have not managed to fix the water supply on our pontoon so they have taken a hose across from the next pontoon, nothing is too much trouble for them. We end the evening chatting with Inge - a Swede sailing alone.

*Roomassaare Yacht Harbour, Estonia*

58°34'.50N / 23°30'.68E – 61NM

## Friday 3rd July

It takes ages to get away - a weather forecast has been obtained for us (but turns out to be inaccurate). A bright sunny day with at first a gentle NW wind. We have to go further out than the fairway buoy to avoid fishing nets and, due to the lack of a detailed chart, we have to go south of the island of Arbruka - it is too risky to take the channel between islands. The wind steadily increases and, by the

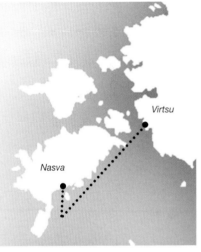

*Virtsu, Estonia - yacht moorings now fitted with metal booms*

time we enter Moon Sound it is NW F5-6 - two reefs in the main and most of the genoa rolled away. The sea develops a nasty short chop. We have two choices of harbour - the ferry ports of Kuivastu and Virtsu either side of the Sound. Reports about the former are that it is officially "closed for rebuilding", being no more than a concrete wall with bits of rusty iron protruding - but boats do visit and are charged for the 'privilege'.

We opt for Virtsu where we find the 'facilities' consist of a rusty pontoon and a few stern buoys - there is little shelter; the outer harbour is for ferries while yachts go further in behind another ferry jetty. It is already overfull and we have to

**CRUISING INFORMATION REPORT**

**VIRTSU**

*A ferry harbour on the east side of the southern end of Moon Sound with berthing for yachts behind the ferry terminal. Exposed to winds from all northerly directions. Berthing - two pontoons at right angles to the jetty with booms (tiny fingers of metal with a floating buoy under the end). Boats can tie alongside the outer pontoon but are then totally exposed to winds blowing down the Sound. The water is shallow at the innermost berths. Water and electricity on the pontoon - need own hose for water. Toilets and showers in the ferry terminal building where there is also a small cafe. Small general store and bank a short distance along the road.*

lay a stern anchor - for which we are not readily equipped. With the help of willing hands and the loan of a dinghy we manage to moor up. The wind is blowing straight down the Sound and across the boats. We have another stressful and uncomfortable night, with little sleep, Utklippan again.

*Virtsu - yacht moorings behind the ferry terminal*

## *Saturday 4th July*

The wind increases to a F6-7. Those going south mostly depart but not without considerable trauma - one gets a line round his prop. Again willing hands help us recover our anchor and move further in where there is slightly better shelter. We also manage to purchase another Russian chart from one of the Finns going south so we are now better equipped to cope with Moon Sound. Despite the high wind, the sun shines all day, we look round ashore then take the ferry across to Muhu Island to see the alternative "harbour" of Kuivastu - merely a concrete wall with bits of rusty iron protruding - and providing no shelter from winds of any southerly direction. As evening approaches the wind dies down and boats are comfortable once more. Many more arrive - Finns are pouring south for their annual holidays. We spend the evening with Ulla and Kalevi from Helsinki who have a converted fishing boat - Novus.

*Virtsu*

*Kuivastu - terminal for the ferries across Moon Sound (mainland to island of Muhu)*
*- no fit place for yachts*

## Virtsu to Haapsalu

58°57'.53N / 23°31'.63E – 37NM

### Sunday 5th July

There is almost no wind - just a light NW F2. This suits us as, for once, we wish to motor - we are voyaging through the notorious Moon Sound where constant and accurate navigation is necessary - we really have no time to deal with sails. Moon Sound was totally forbidden during Soviet times - it is believed that the Russians had dumped all manner of things here or filled it with wrecks but, on a day of brilliant sunshine, it is all very pretty, islands with sandy or reeded shores.

Haapsalu, Estonia - Yacht Club Harbour packed to capacity during the Muhu Vain Regatte

The channel is often shallow, narrow and boulder strewn - good visibility is necessary as you have to follow leading marks - straying off the leading line can bring disaster. In Haapsalu we find the facilities are very much better - a number of quays with stern to buoys although quite exposed to winds from anything in the north. The town lies about a mile away; its main feature a ruined castle attached to which is an intact cathedral - scene of the "White Lady" legend. It is said that a monk from the cathedral fell in love with a young village maiden and smuggled her into the cathedral disguised as a choir boy. When their secret was discovered the monk was thrown into the cellar and the unfortunate girl walled up alive. Known as "The White Lady", her ghost appears at the south window of the baptistry during the moonlit nights of August.

There is also the railway museum - the original impressive railway station in the grand style of Imperial Russia, now disused but a number of traditional steam engines together with diesels and coaches remain. Water pumps are a frequent sight at street corners - very handy for washing ice cream from sticky fingers. The town is a mixture of traditional painted timber houses (Estonian) and ugly concrete structures (Soviet). The Yacht Club is Scandinavian in style, but hideous and broken down concrete structures are in evidence too. Sailing is popular in Estonia although most of the yachts appear to belong to clubs. This week a race is taking place - the Muhu Väin regatte.

**CRUISING INFORMATION REPORT**

*HAAPSALU*

The approach channel to Haapsalu is long and winding but well marked with buoys and leading marks. A 2m draft vessel can easily enter, the shallowest part being beside the harbour itself. There is no shelter from NE to E and in strong wind conditions the harbour can become very uncomfortable or even dangerous. Mooring is by stern buoys bows on to the main quay. Boats with shallower draft can pick their way further in. Water and electricity on quay. Toilets, showers, restaurant and bar at Yacht Club. There is no diesel available at the harbour - it has to be brought by can from one of two garages which both lie on roads leading out from the other side of the town. The harbour is located about 11/2 km from the town. Take bus (No 2) from the end of the short lane leading from the yacht club gate. All facilities in the town, several good and well stocked supermarkets, banks, restaurants, post office etc.

NB - as you approach the harbour, a large notice tells you that you must report in and out to the Border Guards. This procedure is no longer necessary and the notice can be safely ignored.

*Haapsalu - railway museum*

83

*In 1999 we hired a car in Haapsalu and took the ferry to the Island of Hiiumaa (pronounced he-oom-aah).*

The first ferry leaves at 0500, the next at 1030 so we have to get up at 0330! Fortunately it is light at that hour. On Hiiumaa the tarmac road mostly follows the coast around the island - there are no roads across the interior. Forest, mostly deciduous, covers much of the island.

ESTONIA

LATVIA

LITHUANIA

BELARUS

RUSSIA

Hiiumaa

Virtsu

Nasva

*Hiiumaa - the hill of crosses*

*Hiiumaa - coastal boulder marked with water levels, after the great floods of 1893 and 1967*

We visit all the harbours listed in *Mini Loots* and some others listed in the Finnish Guide: - Heltermaa the ferry terminal - untenable in northerly winds, Lehtma untenable in southerly winds, Suursadam full of dying fishing craft and have to conclude that, although work has been done to improve the pontoons and stern buoys in some harbours, there are none that provide safety in all weathers. We also visit Hiiumaa's tourist spots: the huge coastal boulder at Kardla which is marked with lines showing the height of the Baltic sea in the terrible storms of 1893 and 1967; the Hill of Crosses which commemorates the Swedes who were deported to Ukraine in 1781. Where it has become the tradition for visitors to leave a cross somewhere near the monument.

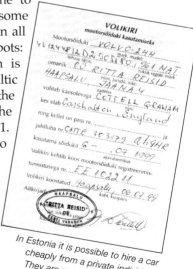

We also drove to the mainland harbours of Dirhami and Paldiski. Dirhami provides only a high concrete quay with great black fenders. Paldiski Nord has a similar quay and here everything is very dirty: stacks of wood line the quay awaiting shipment but, as an emergency port of refuge, this harbour provides shelter.

## Haapsalu to Lohusalu

59°24'.16N / 24°12'.26E – 50NM

*Monday 6th July 1998*

The passage between the island of Vormsi and the mainland is said to be the narrowest part of the channel but, in good visibility and making use of the excellent leading marks, we pick our way safely through and enter the Gulf of Finland - we are now able to sail in a gentle S F2. This dies away and ahead we can see white horses. As we round Paldiski point we are hit by a strong head wind which lasts until we have tied up in Lohusalu. Here we find another excellent little harbour which has recently been dredged. There is good shelter, sufficient room and the usual bows to quay, stern buoy system. There is little here other than the yacht club and another restaurant - the YC is full so we eat at the little restaurant - an excellent meal for very little money.

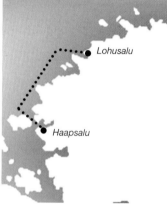

*Lohusalu - small modern marina with a few visitors' spaces*

## Lohusalu to Tallinn

59°27'.99N / 24°49'.70E  – 23NM

*Tuesday 7th July*

As we approach we are in brilliant sunshine but the beautiful spires of Tallinn are obliterated by a thunderstorm and down-pour - which misses us altogether! We enter Pirita Marina - built by the Russians for the 1980 Olympics. It is large but crowded - we see KAOS II tied up to a finger pontoon but we continue through to the Kalev Yacht Club where we manage to find a space between two Estonian yachts. The Harbour Master (carrying a Union Jack) immediately comes out to welcome us to Tallinn. We call at the chandler to purchase a chart to give us the detail of the entry to Helsinki. Yet another shock - no charts. It is the same story here: the Estonian charts (based on the Russian surveys) are no longer being produced.

*Tallinn - Pirita Marina - buildings from the 1980 Olympics*

## Tallinn

*Wednesday 8th to*
*Saturday 11th July*

This is the capital of Estonia and nearly half the total population of about $1^1/_2$ million lives in and around the town. We travel to town by bus (Pirita is a village east of Tallinn). Tallinn old town is large and beautiful - another member of the former Hanseatic League with narrow winding streets and buildings clinging to the steep hillsides.

Tallinn

*Tallinn - Alexander Nevsky cathedral*

*Tallinn - street scene*

A vista of red rooves and spires is provided from a viewpoint at the top of Toompea. Estonia has been under German, Danish, Swedish, Tsarist Russian and, last of all, Soviet Russian rule - all the while the Estonians were only serfs - a history reflected in the buildings. By contrast the suburbs are ugly and run down - the usual post-Soviet mess.

*The red rooves of Tallinn viewed from Toompea*

ESTONIA

### CRUISING INFORMATION REPORT

#### *TALLINN*

*Yachts berth at Pirita, a village 6 km from the town of Tallinn and the site of the marina built by the Russians for the 1980 Olympics. Within the one complex are situated both Pirita Marina and the Kalev Yacht Club. Mooring is by stern buoys. If arriving in late evening and finding the harbour full it is normal to anchor within the harbour and find the first available space next morning. Large vessels can be accommodated in a separate basin in the outer harbour. Water and electricity on quays, toilets and showers in main building. Diesel from Neste station in outer harbour. Chandlers and small supermarket within complex. All facilities in Tallinn - frequent buses from Pirita.*

*Tallinn - the wall of sweaters*

# FINLAND

## Tallinn to Helsinki

60°09'.62N / 24°57'.85E – 49NM

*Sunday 12th July*

The Border Control and Customs Office opens at 0800 - there is a queue of boats waiting to leave but the formalities do not take long. As we leave the harbour it seems the wind (forecast to be SE) will be behind us but as we leave the shelter of the Estonian Islands we quickly discover we have a NE F5 and we are only just able to make

Helsinki

Tallinn

the course for Helsinki.
Under foresail alone we are making over 7kts and keeping pace with Finnish boats returning home. The sea is mountainous and we are constantly shipping water. It is so rough that navigation becomes a problem - particularly in the unfamiliar rock-strewn entrance to Helsinki.

*Tallinn - Aviator's monument beside the road from Pirita to Tallinn*

90

Gaining some confidence from the Finnish boats around us who (hopefully) know their way home - gradually the sea lessens and then we find some shelter from the islands, but the wind never abates - in fact it increases to a F6 in the final approaches. The skyline of Helsinki looks interesting and the island scenery - rose - coloured rock topped with trees and little red houses - is most attractive. Passport Control and Customs - is located on the fortress island of Soumenlinna where there is a sheltered natural harbour. Again the formalities do not take long and we proceed to the Nyländska Jaktklubben (NJK) whose premises, at Blekholmen in South Harbour are frequently used by visiting yachtsmen. In brilliant sunshine this is a very attractive setting, an elegant clubhouse on a tiny tree topped island (with a ferry to town), berthing is a mixture of stern buoys and finger pontoons. Now it is time to phone home - whilst we swelter in hot sunshine, it turns out that the rain is pouring down in England!

*Tallinn to Helsinki hydrofoil*

**Helsinki**

## Monday 13th to Friday 17th July

Helsinki is a mass of islands joined by bridges. It has been Finland's capital since 1812. The city centre is compact, a grid system with substantial well-to-do buildings. The skyline is dominated by the green domes of the Lutheran cathedral in Senate Square. The interior is plain as all Lutheran churches - by contrast the interior of the Russian Orthodox Uspensky Cathedral is filled with gold leaf and beautiful icons. At South Harbour there is an excellent open air market with stalls under orange awnings selling everything from mountains of local grown strawberries, cherries, peas, mushrooms to smoked fish and souvenirs - to furs. There is also a covered market hall with stalls providing smoked fish, meat, vegetables, chocolates. Leading from the market place is Esplanadi - a wide street with a tree-lined park area down the centre with

Helsinki

ESTONIA

Helsinki - NJK yacht club on Blekholmen, South Harbour

Helsinki - Sibelius monument

Helsinki - strawberries and much more for sale
in South Harbour market

restaurants and a stage where a variety of entertainment is provided free. One evening we watch a display of Finnish folk dancing. A Helsinki Card gives unlimited travel on the city's buses, trams and metro plus a guided bus tour of the town, various boat trips - to the island fortress of Soumenlinna, free entry to several art galleries and museums. The sale of alcohol in Finland is state controlled - here the shops are called "Alko" which we find to be large supermarkets crammed with every conceivable alchoholic drink - at prices on a par with the UK.

Helsinki - Lutheran Cathedral dominating Senate Square

59°58'.74N / 23°53'.13E – 41NM

## Saturday 18th July

It is time to make a move but at least here in the Baltic boats do not grow weed whilst standing idle. Our antifouling is as clean as the day we painted it - but we have a line of oil gathered in Tallinn which we need to scrub and many brown stains on the hull (which can easily be removed with oxalic acid). Leif Strandstrom, the Harbour Master at the NJK Yacht Club, Helsinki, has recommended some likely harbours on our route west and we set off for Jakobshamn in a light N/NWIy. Navigation through the islands is by "leads" - extremely well marked with leading marks and buoys. All day we follow channels on leading marks, some are two black and white boards, white sides

*Typical scene amongst the islands - Finnish archipelago*

with a black stripe down the middle, others (more common) are yellow with a red central stripe. Most have lights. You either line up two boards so the centre stripe appears as one continuous vertical line or line up the two boards so that the back board is obscured by the front board. The upkeep of all the buoys and markers is paid for by general taxation - they are considered necessary for commercial craft as well as pleasure boats - but in a land where so many own boats, few will grumble. There are also small white cairns and white painted marks on rocks, these are to line up the buoys, which may move during winter ice and storms. However, as the EU does not require leading marks, we are told that the Finnish Government is no longer going to maintain them; they will not repair them when damaged. Conversely, the Government is so confident of its marks that it will pay for your damage should you hit a rock whilst on a leading line.

In the warm sunshine and brilliant blue sky, the scenery is beautiful - thousands of little islands topped with fir trees, some with pink rock shores others with reeded shores, the little red summer house much in evidence among the trees. The air is clear and visibility excellent - at one time we "identify" a small town but on closer inspection this turns out to be a fleet of sailing dinghies out racing. There are many other boats about and having once again become accustomed to following the leads we have a pleasant day. Finland has a population of around 5 million - it seems a large proportion must own boats There is a strong wind forecast and we feel that Jakobshamn may be exposed so we find a sheltered anchorage above the ferry at Barösund where the channel between islands is quite narrow and we can anchor in a pool. The evening is warm and pleasant, a barbecue is a must, we have had few this during this cruise thanks to the weather.

*Sunset in the Finnish archipelago*

## Barösund to Ekenäs

59°58'.66N / 23°25'.76E  –  29NM

*Sunday 19th July*

So far the forecast of F7 with rain has not materialised so we set off once more between the islands. The bright morning becomes cloudy and the westerly wind increases but is still moderate until we have tied up in Ekenäs (Finnish name Tammisaari) Leif also recommended this as an interesting town to visit. As we approach, the sun again comes out making the scenery most attractive.

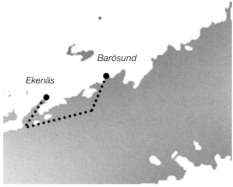

*Ekenäs (Tammisaari) - yacht moorings and harbour - restaurant built on piles*

There is a mixture of boxes (apparently only for local boats!), a few alongside berths and several stern buoys - we have the luck to find one vacant space among the latter although there are now three boats on the buoy. Everyone is so welcoming - we are helped in and our lines taken. One neighbour has recently returned from the south coast of England and says the weather was terrible, the other welcomes us to Finland. We take a stroll round the town - not particularly old but the residential areas are mainly painted timber clad houses of a similar style to the Baltic States but all well kept and smart - no peeling paint here. A particular landmark of the town is a restaurant on stilts just outside the yacht harbour. The Town Council turned down the original owner's application to build a restaurant in the town on the grounds that

*Ekenäs Church*

there were already too many restaurants. Not deterred, the restauranteur went ahead with his plans and built his restaurant outside the town - 'on the water'. By evening the wind has risen - a westerly F5/6 and the air is cold.

*Ekenäs - Church and houses  rebuilt after a great fire*

Ekenäs

*Monday 20th July*

In the town the timber clad houses are painted in a variety of colours with the window frames and borders picked out in white. In lands where there is plenty of timber it makes sense to build houses of wood but in nearly every town we visit history records some disastrous fire - Ekenäs is no exception - their fire burnt down the church and neighbouring houses. The church was rebuilt of stone but the houses are still wooden - only now the streets are wider. Streets are

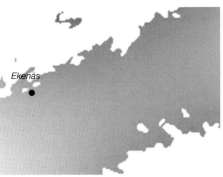

Ekenäs

named after the professions of their inhabitants: hat maker's street, glovers street, linen weavers etc. In the old market square stands the pillory - the neck chain is original, though the wooden post has been replaced. Finland is officially bilingual although only 5% of the total population is Swedish-speaking. However in Ekenäs the majority of the population is Swedish-speaking thus signs and street names tend to be in Swedish first, Finnish second.

Perhaps this is not surprising as the town was founded in 1546 by the Swedish King Gustav Vasa.

*Ticket for Hanko Water Tower*

### Ekenäs to Hanko

59°49′.16N / 22°58′.02E – 22NM

*Tuesday 21st July*

The wind has subsided somewhat so we set off mid morning in company with many others. It is bright and sunny but the Wly wind (on the nose) is cold. We follow leads and leading marks and buoyed channels like corkscrews on tortuous paths between rocks. Hanko is Finland's most southerly port and longest ice free. It is a commercial port and railway town. We find an old steam engine - a museum piece - parked near the station - the skipper fulfils every small boy's dream of having his photo taken in the cab. The old town contains the usual timber clad houses but the newer town is concrete and ugly. This was a favourite spa of

*Hanko - the water tower*

*Hanko - view from the water tower showing yacht harbour and part of the archipelago*

Russian aristocracy in the 19th century and the elegant villas they built still grace the eastern side of the town. For FIM5 we take the lift up the water tower and have a spectacular view over the town and surrounding countryside. Below is a vista of pinetrees stretching as far as the eye can see inland with here and there a chimney or industrial plant sticking through the top and on the coast thousands of islands with boats threading their way along the leads. Hanko yacht harbour is large but very full - mostly Finns and a few Swedes, an occasional German and one boat from Latvia. At the

**CRUISING INFORMATION REPORT**

*HANKO*

*(Swedish - Hangö)*
*150 visitors' berths - located on most pontoons in the harbour (the sailing club owns the pontoons farthest in) - berthing by stern buoys. Water and electricity on pontoon. Diesel from fuel berth in harbour. Full facilities in town.*

tourist office we are immediately informed of the kiosk which sells the largest ice creams in Finland - this has to be our first stop!

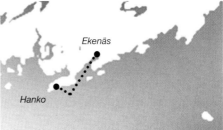

*Hanko - the skipper in charge of a museum piece*

# Hanko to Högsåra

59°57'.77N / 22°21'.74E – 25NM

## *Wednesday 22nd July*

The day starts misty... we cannot see across the harbour - this is quite a surprise in a land where clear air and excellent visibility are the norm. The mist gradually clears while we spend the morning writing letters. According to Finnish folklore, in this last week of July a witch throws a cold stone into the water and that is the beginning of the end of summer. The waterstand is very high - 40 cm (16") - due to the constant bad weather and persistent strong winds. We indulge in another huge ice cream and buy strawberries and peas at a stall on the quayside. Strawberries etc are sold by the litre  - scooped up into a jug-like measure - thus if you buy the smaller sweeter berries more fit into the jug, and stretch the tummy elastic to the limit.  In a light easterly we sail with mainsail alone - the foresail obscures visibility. Again  we are following  leads  between rocks and islands - it is so well marked that you would have to be stupid or very unlucky to have an accident but sometimes the route takes you nerve wrackingly close to rocks. As the afternoon progresses the sky clouds over and a few spots of rain are felt but as we approach our chosen anchorage the clouds disappear, the sun  comes out and we can enjoy another barbecue and fill ourselves with strawberries.

*Typical scene in the Finnish archipelago*

# Högsåra to Gullkrona

60°05′.34N / 22°04′.90E – 15NM

*Thursday 23rd July*

**CRUISING INFORMATION REPORT**

***GULLKRONA***

*Private island belonging to the Eriksson family. Berthing - stern anchor - bows to pontoon or anchor in pool. One harbour fee covers all visits in same season.*

A peaceful night, several other boats also drop anchor, the harbour has one pontoon which is full. In the morning when several boats have left we move over to the pontoon and moor up with bow anchor and stern to quay. This enables us to have a short walk round the wooded island where we find the usual museum depicting Finnish life, here mostly with pictures. The wind is SW/W3/4, the sea

*Gullkrona - TAM O'SHANTER at anchor*

*Gullkrona - some of the trolls on the nature trail*

sometimes choppy with white horses but even with many twists and turns to our route, the wind will let us sail. We arrive in the sheltered anchorage of Gullkrona just after lunch. The harbour facilities are pontoons using stern anchor - we cannot face our anchor being entangled with all the others so anchor off and go ashore by dinghy. This is a private island belonging to the Eriksson family. There is a fish shop-cum-harbour office, some summer houses, a sauna, a restored post windmill and an old pilot cottage. We walk round the nature trail where ingenious and amusing faces have been painted on bits of fallen tree and rocks - every one different. There is the usual "museum" with artefacts from everyday life - some look familiar!

*Gullkrona - windmill*

## Gullkrona to Turku

60°26'.45N / 22°14'.89E – 25NM

### *Friday 24th July*

We sail all the way, even straight from the anchorage. We always seem to meet up with a tug and a tow - one passes us at a bend in the channel but we manage to keep out of its way. Soon afterwards at a wider place we see another tug towing two platforms with lifting gear followed by a long line of floats - perhaps a pipeline. We wonder how it will get through the twisting channel without destroying the buoys. It is a sunny morning but by mid afternoon again clouds are gathering on the horizon. We follow the narrow channel to Turku. Along the banks are splendid houses, people wave to us from their jetties. A pleasant surprise is to find Novus - and there is a vacant berth beside her. Later we walk along the quay-side and find the strangest thing - the "Leningrad Dixieland Jazz Band" - eight pretty good musicians from Russia playing traditional jazz in Finland, and they are much appreciated. We talk to the banjo player who knows some English.

*Turku - international flags fly over the visitors' berths*

# Turku

## Saturday 25th/
## Monday 27th July

Turku is Finland's second city and former capital. It too suffered a disastrous fire and was rebuilt around 1827. The town straddles the River Aura with the streets rising on either side. The river bank is tree lined and pleasant - mostly limes whose scent fills the air. The main part of the town lies on the west bank. It is another grid -pattern town with most of the buildings being at best boring. There are many shops with expensive goods, several supermarkets and both an indoor and outdoor market. The 13th century cathedral, set in a small park beside the river, is large, old and interesting - there are some almost obliterated wall paintings but, if one stands quietly studying them, letting one's eyes become accustomed to the

*Turku Castle*

*Turku - Soumen Joutsen - Swan of Finland*

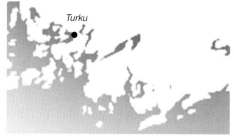

*Turku*

FINLAND

ESTONIA

dim light, images begin to appear - no doubt the old paint stained the fabric of the stone. In the area near the cathedral some large and imposing buildings remain - presumably from the Russian Tsarist era. Near the harbour entrance lies Turku Castle dating from around 1280. Just above the yacht harbour a little passenger ferry plies back and forth all day - totally free. Further along the river bank the frigate SUOMEN JOUTSEN (Swan of Finland) is moored - built in France in 1902 it is now a museum. Our harbour fee is FIM 70 (£7.78) per day - which includes electricity, water, sauna (which we both try) showers, loos and free laundry facilities. Sunday is my birthday and messages arrive from England, Turkey and the Netherlands. In the afternoon we take a train ride (at FIM 25 each, expensive compared with the harbour fee) to Naantali a short distance up the coast - another attractive little town with a large number of old timber houses - and on the hill above St Brigid's convent church. Naantali, once a favourite holiday retreat of the Tzar, is now famous for 'Moominworld' - a sort of Scandinavian Disneyworld.

*Naantali — historic village and popular weekend harbour for Finnish sailors. One summer the harbour fees were greatly increased so the harbour was boycotted — the shopkeepers protested at their loss of livelihood — and the prices had to come down again!*

## Turku to Kyrkbacken (Nagu Island)

60°11'.69N / 21°54'.79E – 20NM

*Tuesday 28th July*

After Monday's rain this is definitely a better day - warm sunshine and no wind. A French couple moored nearby tell us they have kept their boat in the Baltic over several winters and give us a few tips on successful winterisation (not least the best way to store wine!). Another British boat has

**CRUISING INFORMATION REPORT**

***KYRKBACKEN (NAGU ISLAND)***

*The guest harbour has a number of pontoons, mostly with stern buoys. Water and electricity on pontoon, showers, toilets, laundry at harbour office. Diesel from fuel pontoon. General stores, bank and restaurants ashore.*

appeared in the marina - an almost new Swan - we have a short chat on the quay-side before our departure. There are two fuel pontoons at the mouth of the river and we stop briefly to refuel. As we make our way down the long straight channel leading from Turku the air is so clear that every detail - boats, trees, houses, is

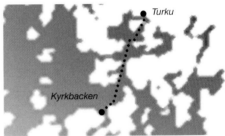

*Tug with two tows - Finnish archipelago*

easily visible over a distance of more than 10 miles. We are beginning to notice though that, even in July, the sun is becoming much lower in the sky. Chris from Kaos II rings - they have now reached Mariehamn and will soon be making for Sweden and the Göta Canal. As we have now decided to leave the boat in the Stockholm area, we have more time to spend in the islands so there is no chance we will catch up. Whilst we are in the archipelago we are able to travel short distances - perhaps 15 miles each day - there are so many suitable anchorages both natural harbours and small villages with pontoons. By mid afternoon we arrive in Kyrkbacken - a holiday resort with a marina, restaurants, supermarkets - and a couple of churches. The graveyard at the Lutheran church is beautifully kept and we notice that there are more Swedish than Finnish family names on the grave stones. The Navtex, which received nothing whilst we were in Turku, is working again - it immediately picks up a gale warning for all the local sea areas! The marina is crowded - more boats arrive by the minute. We are anchored at one side of the bay and hope we will have sufficient shelter.

## Wednesday 29th to Thursday 30th July

There is horizontal rain all day and the wind picks up from the N/NE - if it goes more northerly we will have to move. Boats are still pouring into the marina - a few leave but space runs out and the Harbour Master puts some yachts beside the ferry pontoon. By Thursday the wind has become S/SW but still strong. At least the day is sunny and we can get ashore - there is another Brit in the harbour - a boat from Jersey. Some time is spent repairing a cut in the dinghy floor. By evening it is raining once more and continues during the night. Television news shows strawberries drowning in their beds - perhaps we have seen and eaten the last.

*Sheltered anchorage in popular natural harbour on island of Björkö*

## Kyrkbacken to Vadviken (Houtskär Island)

60°12'.26N / 21°22'.62E – 20NM

### Friday 31st July

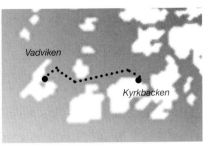

It is still windy but less than the previous days. We have the conflict of remaining in a safe anchorage yet another day or moving on. We opt for moving on and sail under reduced sail in a south westerly F4/5 gusting 6. We are always in the shelter of the islands and there is no fetch and no waves. Just before the entrance channel to our chosen stopping place we see a tug and a tow - timber - anchored in the shelter of an island - presumably even its powerful engine is no match for today's wind. We find a beautiful sheltered anchorage at the head of a bay and drop anchor just as a rainshower descends.

*Quiet mooring in the Finnish archipelago*

# ÅLAND ISLANDS

## Vadviken to Torsholm (Kumlinge Island)

60°17'.36N / 20°47'.21E – 25 NM

*Saturday 1st August*

A very dull start but the wind has now eased to a southerly F3/4 gusting 5. At Näsby where we stop in the hope of replenishing our ice cream the only shop is crowded and with long queues. We sail on into the Sea of Åland by more narrow channels between rocky islets. We are now in the Åland Islands proper and raise the Åland Islands courtesy flag - blue background with yellow and red crosses superimposed. Vimpels in these colours fly from the flagpoles of houses on the islands. The sun shines most of the day - the scenery is beautiful - here the islands are smaller and lower. We find a pleasant anchorage in a bay just beyond

a ferry terminal (ferries link most of the islands). We arrive by mid afternoon so have time to row ashore and walk along a pink granite road. Wild strawberries grow in profusion by the roadside - there are plenty for us and the birds. Wild flowers, butterflies and dragonflies abound. The islands are heavily wooded and there are real Christmas trees (the Norway Spruce) growing wild.

*Finnish archipelago - little red houses*

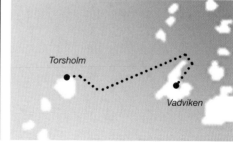

## Torsholm to Norviken, Bomarsund

60°13'.25N / 20°13'.99E – 31NM

*Sunday 2nd August*

A totally frustrating day - whenever we think to sail the wind heads us within seconds and we have to motor. It is too dangerous to tack as it is imperative to keep to the leads and on the leading lines. Some sun, some cloud but the wind is cold. The islands are lower and less treeclad, but we are at the same latitude as Shetland so wonder how the trees grow at all. As we join yet another channel between islands, we meet the same tug and tow we saw anchored a few days ago - but now there are two barges of wood in tow. We arrive at Bomarsund by late afternoon anticipating tying up to a quay with water and electricity available. When we arrive however the harbour is packed and there are dinghies racing all over the place - there is an international scout jamboree with 1,500 scouts gathered. The wind is forecast to turn easterly so we seek shelter at one side of the

bay anchoring fore and aft - much easier now we have a stern anchor reel which we can use with either anchor or stern hook.

*Dead on the line - leading marks in the Finish archipelago*

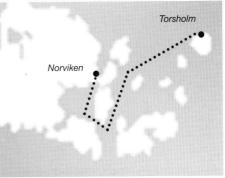

60°12'.50N / 20°05'.00E – 15NM

## Monday 3rd August

It has been a peaceful night and, in the morning sunshine, we row ashore. Little remains of the fortress - built by the Russians over a period of 10 years, it was destroyed by a British and French fleet in two days in 1854 at the time of the Crimean war. From the remaining ruins it can be seen to have been a huge fort. We sail slowly and lazily towards Kastelholm but find there is a 19m overhead power cable across the channel below the harbour. Our air draught is 18.3m so we decide not to take the risk and anchor in a bay about a mile short. It is hot and sunny and we go up the creek by dinghy. Here we find the remains of a huge 14th century Swedish castle which was destroyed by fire in the 19th century and is now being restored. This is also the site of a recon-structed island village - houses brought from all over and rebuilt in Jan Karlsgården. There are several windmills, houses and byres, corn stores and a smithy plus a village pond. We also find the best example of a Midsummer pole we have yet seen. We had hoped to find a shop but again there is only a kiosk.

*Bomarsund, Åland Islands - ruins of fortress in background*

## Kastelholm to Mariehamn

60°06′.05N / 19°56′.85E – 13NM

*Tuesday 4th August*

Another blow is forecast so we will be glad to be in harbour at Mariehamn for a few days. It is but a short distance across the lake-like Lumparn from where we follow a narrow waterway leading to the Lemströms canal and the 'back door' to Mariehamns Eastern Harbour. There is a swing bridge over the canal opening every hour on the hour — on demand — over a 10 minute period. The times we had been told were incorrect so we miss the opening and anchor (using lead weights) for a short time. A Finn anchored nearby comes over in his dinghy to chat. Once through the bridge we have only to pass round an island and Mariehamn's Eastern Harbour lies before us. Mariehamn is built on a narrow peninsular and has harbours on both east and west - east is most sheltered. There is plenty of space - not so many boats about now - we again use the stern buoy system but the pontoon is very low and it is quite a struggle to get on and off over the bow. Soon after we arrive the

Kastelholm, Aland - summer poles remain standing all year

Kastelholm

Mariehamn

wind rises and drizzle starts - almost obliterating the landscape but we manage to get ashore - the town is very close and we seek out the supermarkets - we ran out of ice cream two days ago so the situation is becoming desperate! We walk across to the Western harbour (where the ferries come in) - wind and waves are sweeping straight in making it an uncomfortable place.

*Entrance to the Lemstroms Canal the 'back door' to Mariehamn's easter harbour, Åland*

## Mariehamn

## Wednesday 5th to Tuesday 11th August

The Åland Islands comprise more than 6,000 islands with a history of habitation going back to pre-Roman times. They were part of Sweden until the early 1800s when Sweden was forced to relinquish Finland and Åland to Russia. Åland then became part of the Grand Duchy of Finland thus part of the Russian Empire. The population is Swedish speaking and their culture closely resembles that of Sweden. When the Russian Empire disintegrated after the revolution of 1917, Finland declared itself independent but the Islanders wished to rejoin Sweden.

*THE POMMERN - permanently moored in Mariehamn's western harbour*

### CRUISING INFORMATION REPORT

#### MARIEHAMN

*Mariehamn is on a peninsular with harbours on East and West. At Eastern Harbour (MSF sailing club) the visitors berths are in the northern section of the harbour - berthing a mixture of stern posts and stern buoys. Harbour captain Ove Sundblom. At Western Harbour, (Åss Marina) berthing is by stern buoy to a number of long pontoons. Harbour Captain Raphael Karlsson. For both harbours - water and electricity on pontoon, showers, toilets, laundry in harbour building. Diesel from fuel berth. All facilities, shops, banks, post office etc in town. Included in your harbour fee, for each night of your stay, is a free ticket for skipper and crew to take a duty free cruise to Sweden and back either from Mariehamn to Kapellskär Eckerö to Grisslehamn.*

The League of Nations however decided that the they should be under Finnish sovereignty but with safeguards as regards language and demilitarised and neutral status. Today Åland even has its own registration numbers for cars and issues its own stamps.

Mariehamn, the capital, was founded in 1861 by Tzar Alexander II and named after his wife Maria Alexandrovna. There were then 33 inhabitants - now there are more than 10,000 - the total island population is around 25,000. The shopping centre of Mariehamn is grid pattern and somewhat characterless - we are told the old houses were knocked down and more modem concrete structures erected. The outskirts are pleasant with older buildings and wide, tree-lined streets - it is called the "town of a thousand lindens" (limes).

With our duty-free ticket we travel to Grisslehamn on the Eckerö Line ferry - a very comfortable bus picks us up at the harbour and takes us the 30 km to the ferry at Eckerö At Eckerö there is a huge former Post and Customs house,dating from the time of the Tzars when mail for St. Petersburg was brought via the Ålands from Stockholm - this impressive building was the first sight travellers had of the Russian Empire. One of Mariehamn's most famous sights is the POMMERN permanently moored in Western Harbour. POMMERM is the only 4 masted barque preserved in its original state. Built by J Reid & Co in Glasgow she was launched in 1903 and originally German owned but later became part of Gustav Erikson's fleet of windjammers sailing the grain trade route between Australia and England. POMMERN is now a museum ship - we spend a couple of hours aboard and still wonder how you would know which "string" to pull to do what (there was a crew of 26)! The main chandlers lies north of the town - a free taxi is provided to take yachtsmen from both harbours.

Stockholm

Free ticket for duty free cruises

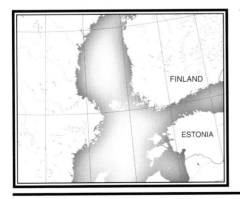

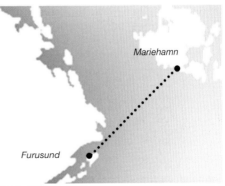

FINLAND

ESTONIA

Mariehamn

Furusund

# FINLAND TO SWEDEN

## Mariehamn to Furusund (Sweden)

59°39'.62N / 18°55'.06E – 48NM

## *Wednesday 12th August*

After more than a week it is time to leave. Although going to another EU country, Finnish rules dictate that all yachts must report out to Passport Control sometimes simply by calling the Coastguard on VHF Ch. 74. A SEly 3-4 picks up and, after leaving the islands, we have one of the best sails this cruise across the Ålands Hav to Sweden. Off the point of Lilla Batskär Island (the Nyhamn light) the chart warns of a magnetic anomaly - even so it is alarming to find oneself 30° off course. The air is crystal clear and visibility excellent - whilst still close to the Åland shore we can pick up a high observation tower on the Swedish coast - which marks the point at which we will enter the archipelago. There is a constant flow of shipping - ferries from Stockholm and Kapellskär to Mariehamn, Turku and Helsinki and commercial traffic up and down the Gulf of Bothnia, including two tugs and tows - the favoured means of moving wood and other heavy loads. After we reach the outer rocks and islands, we sail on for miles until we reach Furusund - a tiny harbour - just a couple of pontoons and a fuel jetty.

### Back in Sweden

Having arrived back in Sweden, we sailed from Furusund to Vaxholm thence to Stockholm where the Water Festival was taking place. After a few days in Stockholm we sailed to Bullandö to make enquiries and arrange winter storage for TAM O' SHANTER. It was now only mid-August and too early to end the season. Therefore we sailed to Sandhamn (the "Cowes of Sweden") at the entrance to the Stockholm archipelago. We then sailed to Nynashamn and on

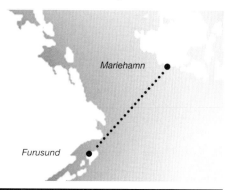

to Södertälje where we entered Lake Mälaren via the Södertälje Canal. In the Lake we explored the island of Björkö, site of an important Viking settlement, stopped in many beautiful and peaceful anchorages, visited Enköping (from where we took a bus to Uppsala) before returning to Stockholm via the Hammerby lock and bridges.

Södertälje — TAM O' SHANTER parked outside McDonalds

By 12th September we arrived back at Bullandö and TAM O'SHANTER was lifted out on the 14th September. We spent nearly a week winterising the boat in a way we had never done before (but can report that all was successful). We hired a car and drove to Göteborg (a journey of some 300 miles - 5 hours) then sailed on the Scandinavian Seaways ferry to Harwich. Family and friends helped us to get our gear back to our home in Fareham.

Ready for winter - TAM O'SHANTER with cockpit cover - hire car packed ready to leave

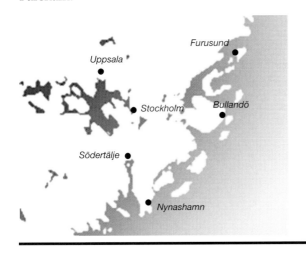

# TAM O'SHANTER
## is a Beneteau
## First 38s5 -

Fin keel, fractional rig
Bermudan sloop
Overall length -
38' (11.7 m)
Draught 6'3"
(2 m approx)
Engine - Volvo 2003

**Sails carried**
Mainsail - with 3 slab
reefs - 38.67sqm
Large genoa (roller
headsail) - 41.82sqm
Working jib
(roller headsail)
Genniker
(furling luff) - 175%
Spinnaker
Trisail
Storm jib

**Ground Tackle**
Main anchor - Delta 16
kg with 30m heavy chain
and 60m warp
Second anchor - Bruce
20kg with 30m chain
and 40m warp
Kedge - Bruce 10kg with
15m chain
and 20m warp
Fisherman
anchor - 7kg

**Liquids Capacity**
Fuel tank capacity -
25 gallons (110lr)
Domestic water tank
capacity - 80 gallons
(360lr) (in 2 tanks)

**Navigational
equipment fitted**
Binnacle compass and
hand bearing compass
Navstar Decca
Raytheon GPS
Autohelm Chartplotter -
world chart and mid-
English Channel detail
chart only - used purely
as a navigation aid and
indicator - navigation
otherwise by traditional
paper chart method
Raytheon radar
Autohelm ST50 - boat
speed, wind speed &
direction, echo sounder,
log and autopilot
Icom VHF
Mapro barometer
and clock
Barograph
NASA Navtex
ICS Navtex

**Other equipment**
Cellnet mobile phone
Domestic radio
Shortwave radio
Laptop computer
and Canon bubblejet
printer
Inboard diesel
generator
Rutland
aerocharger
Ampair
towgen

**Safety equipment**
XM 4-man liferaft
in valise
Life jackets and
safety harnesses
Offshore flare pack
Danbuoy
Lifebuoy and
light tender -
Avon Redcrest
with Tohatsu
3.5 hp outboard

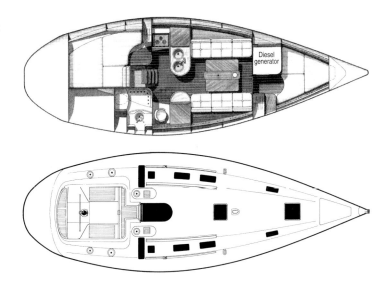

119

# APPENDIX I

# CHARTS

We carried a set of British Admiralty charts for the areas cruised. However, it should be noted that chart numbers and content vary from time to time and anyone wishing to follow in our footsteps would be advised to consult an up to date British Admiralty list.

In addition to the BA charts, which were mostly used for passage making, it is essential to have detailed local charts. This is particularly relevant for the Netherlands and parts of Denmark and absolutely essential for the Swedish and Finnish archipelagos and the waters around Estonia (Moon Sound in particular). It is also important to acquire charts before setting out - we relied on obtaining Estonian charts when we arrived and this proved impossible. Even for Sweden one cannot rely on required charts being in stock in every port.

### Sweden
Swedish Small Craft Charts - in book form

| | |
|---|---|
| A | Stockholm's Skärgård |
| C | Ostkusten |
| D | Mälaren |
| F | Sydostkusten |

### Finland
Finnish Small Craft Charts - in book form

| | |
|---|---|
| Z | Pellinki to Inkoo |
| B | Jussarö to Parainen |
| D | Turun to Saaristo |
| C | Åland |

### Estonia/Latvia

NB  Both the Estonian and Latvian Hydrographic Offices publish charts but at the time of our cruise, complete coverage was not available. Much effort is being put in by these authorities and the situation is rapidly improving.

We used the following charts:
Atlas for Small Craft Tallinn to Riga [believed to be out of print - summer 2000]
Russian charts for Moon Sound Estonia (Muhu Vain)
23063    Estonia Moon Sound
27025    Estonia Telisnaneem to Rukikirahusaar
(large scale chart of sound between island of Vormsi and mainland Estonia)

# PILOT BOOKS

**Cruising Germany and Denmark**
Brian Navin, Imray 1994
**The Baltic Sea**  Barry Sheffield, RCC Pilotage Foundation, pub Imray, 1992
**Cruising Association Handbook** - 8th edition
**Swedish Kusthandbok series**
(in Swedish but with good harbour photos)
**Naturhamnar pa Ostkusten** (Natural Harbours of the East Coast of Sweden) - Ameen/Hansson
(in Swedish but with good  harbour plans)
**Gästhamns Guiden** - Swedish Harbour Guide - published annually and free from Chandlers, Yacht Clubs and Tourist Offices (in Swedish with harbour photos and glossary of terms in English)
**Svenska KUSTregistret** - general sailing information - in Swedish available free from Chandlers, Yacht Clubs and Tourist Offices
**"Väderkortet"** Pocket size weather cards also available  from Chandlers etc

**Finland -**  until 2000, harbour guides accompanied small craft charts. There is now a harbour guide entitled **Käyntisatamat/Besökshamnar** (in Finnish and Swedish but with harbour plans and symbols for facilities)
**Baltian Satamakirja Viro Latvia Liettua** (Baltic States Harbour Guide in Finnish but with excellent harbour plans)
**Teatmik** - Estonian Harbour Guide (in English and Estonian)
**MiniLoots 1996** - Estonian Harbour Guide (in English , German and Estonian) - now out of date and replaced by Teatmik)
**Latvijas Jahtu Ostas** (Latvian Yacht Harbours) (in English and Latvian)

# APPENDIX II

## WEATHER AND WEATHER FORECASTS

Weather in the Western Baltic is influenced by Atlantic weather systems and as such can be very changeable. However, the further east and north one goes the Atlantic influences are lessened and the weather is influenced more by the land mass of Eastern Europe and summers can be very warm. This in turn can lead to a very high tendency of thunderstorms developing. (Under these conditions you would be well advised to disconnect your aerials from instrumentation).

**Sources of weather information which we have used**

The BBC Shipping Forecast covers all sea areas whilst passage making as far as the Kiel Canal and for more detailed forecasts of specific areas local VHF stations, both marine and land-based exist all along the coast. Some of these transmit in English.

Beyond the Kiel Canal, in the Baltic Sea, again local VHF and marine stations give weather information. Otherwise, the most reliable sources of weather information are Navtex, weather facsimile and radio teletype (RTTY).

**Navtex** Tune to stations U and J.Forecasts are issued twice daily, times as detailed in MacMillans etc.

**Weather facsimile** To receive this you need appropriate receiving equipment whether it be a dedicated set or in conjunction with a single side band short wave radio receiver and computer with appropriate software. The best station to tune to for the Baltic is Hamburg on frequencies 3855 kHz, 7880 kHz and 13882.5 kHz - schedule of transmissions obtainable from the Internet - http://www.dwd.de/services/gfsf/e_faxpln.html.

**RTTY** You need the same equipment as for facsimile above. Again Hamburg is the best station to tune to on frequencies 4583 kHz, 7646 kHz or 10100.8 kHz for programme 1 or 147.3 kHz, 11039 kHz or 14467.3 kHz for programme 2.

Schedule of transmissions obtainable from the Internet - http://www.dwd.de/services/gfsf/e_telexpln.html.

In addition to the above, when sailing in both Sweden and Finland, local weather forecasts are transmitted on marine VHF working channels.

In Sweden, transmissions always come from Stockholm Radio but are broadcast on the appropriate channel for the area in which you are sailing. These follow an announcement on Ch 16. The appropriate channels are detailed in the free booklet Kustregistret. Transmissions are made in both Swedish and English - Caveat - the quoted times for broadcasts in Swedish are in local time whereas those in English are in UTC. Some of the Swedish language forecasts are much more detailed giving expected weather for four periods throughout the 24 hours and including station reports all around the coast. By constant monitoring, sufficient Swedish to usefully interpret the forecast will soon be gained.

In Finland, transmissions come from either Helsinki or Turku Radio (for the area covered by our cruise). Details of transmission times and channels are given in the Finnish Small Craft Charts. Transmissions are first made in English then repeated in Finnish.

In the Baltic States, forecasts are often obtainable from the harbour offices but our experience has shown them to be less reliable than those obtainable by Navtex, weather facsimile or RTTY.

In general in the Baltic countries, wind speed is measured in metres per second. However, in the case of RTTY transmissions received from Hamburg, these are always in Beaufort. A useful approximate conversion is m/s divided by 2 equals Beaufort, or m/s multiplied by 2 equals knots e.g. 10 m/s is equal to F5 or 20 knots.

# APPENDIX III

## FORMALITIES

For the countries covered in this book, no visas are required for British Passport Holders.

**Lithuania**

Visiting yachts are required to report in and out of Klaipeda — Lithuania's only seaport. The Q flag is not used.

**Latvia**

Visiting yachts are required to report in and out of each port visited (note that there is no Border Control Office at Engure, thus no reporting). At Riga the Harbour Office make the report on behalf of yachts unless Riga is the port of entry/exit to/from Latvia. The officials are friendly and welcoming, most have reasonable English. The Q flag is not used.

**Estonia**

It is necessary only to clear in when arriving in the country and out when leaving. Entry/exit therefore has to be at an official port of entry. At present these are:

Nasva/Kuressaare/Roomassaare, Parnu, Ruhnu, Veere, Lehtma, Dirhami, Pirita (Tallinn), Vergi and Narva. Most Border Guards speak good English and are both pleasant and efficient. The Q flag is not used.

**Finland**

When passing between Finland and countries outside the EU, yachts are naturally subject to Immigration and Customs Control. This is carried out at designated Passport Control stations which are located at logical entry places. However, although itself a member of the EU, Finland requires all yachts passing between Finland and other EU countries also to report to Passport Control. In this case it is sometimes possible to report out merely by a VHF call to the local Coastguard on Ch 74 — but check this is acceptable before leaving — you may be called back if not. A crewlist is required when reporting in – at least two copies. The Q flag is not used.

**The following simple crew list is all that is required in both the Baltic States and Finland.**

**CREW LIST**

Yacht Name
Home Port
Registration Number
Last Port of Call
Next Port of Call
Date

| Name | Rank | Nationality | Place and Date of Birth | Passport No |
|------|------|-------------|-------------------------|-------------|
|      |      |             |                         |             |

# APPENDIX IV

# WINTERING IN THE BALTIC

There is a wide choice of boatyards (and possibly even sailing clubs) where boats can be left during the winter. The facilities offered vary - methods of lifting, whether the boats will be outdoors or in a hall, if outdoors whether the mast can be left up or taken down. Depending on location, temperatures can go down to as low as minus 40°C. Finland is much colder than central Sweden and obviously the further south one goes the less severe the temperatures. There are a few places where boats are kept in the water, some are sufficiently far south that the water rarely freezes and in other cases curtains of air bubbles can be arranged to keep the water ice free around the hull. Where boats are stored out of doors, it is essential that they are covered particularly in the cockpit area to prevent the build up of snow and ice causing problems. Boats with wooden decks should be covered overall. Generally it is normal for owners to do all their own work.

## WINTERISATION

### ENGINE AND/OR GENERATOR

Change engine oil - renew primary and secondary fuel filters.

In both fresh water and salt water cooling circuits use antifreeze (ethylene glycol) diluted 1:1 to give maximum protection. (For salt water circuit, remove intake pipe from seacock and place in a container of 1:1 antifreeze - run engine until antifreeze is seen to be ejected from exhaust system and stop engine.)

Spray engine with anticorrosive spray such as WD40.

Block exhaust with rag.

Treat fuel with inhibitor.

Ensure fuel tank is completely full.

### DOMESTIC

Pour 1:1 antifreeze into toilet bowl, bilge pump trough and shower tray and pump through

Release all connections so that no water is trapped.

Empty holding tank, if fitted.

Empty water tanks.

Drain down water system - open all taps to release air locks.

Disconnect pipes at any manifolds and drain.

Drain calorifier (if fitted) - remove maximum amount of water - check by blowing air through both flow and return pipes. A dinghy pump can be useful to start the syphon action and to check that air can be blown through. Some water will always remain in the container but this should not cause a problem provided there is space for the water to expand when it changes to ice on freezing. DO NOT PUT ETHYLENE GLYCOL IN THE CALORIFIER OR FRESH WATER TANKS - THIS IS HIGHLY POISONOUS.

## ELECTRICS

Ensure all batteries are fully charged. If fitted with a wind generator or solar panels isolate batteries and connect power source to positive terminals via blocking diodes so as to keep all batteries isolated but receiving a trickle charge throughout the winter months. Alternatively have the boatyard look after the batteries.

## FIBREGLASS HULLS

Drill hole in bottom of rudder to drain any water (fill hole in Spring.)

## GAS

Ensure gas bottle is shut off and disconnect supply pipe to boat.

## OUTBOARD ENGINE

Run through with fresh water (Baltic Sea is almost salt free). Treat with WD40.
Remove petrol from tank.

## GENERAL

Leave all seacocks open but remember to close before being launched. If seacocks are left closed condensation can build up and break open the fitting on freezing.

The boat must be covered - in the case of fibreglass-decked boats covering the cockpit is sufficient. For boats with wooden decks in all cases the whole boat should be covered. To assist, the boom can be used to support the cover and if possible remove stanchions and guard rails to achieve a better angle for fall off of snow. If the mast is taken off, then a wooden/metal structure must be constructed to support the cover.

If there is no facility to store instrumentation, books and charts, clothes etc ashore then they will survive the winter. The basic difference from UK is that most of the winter the temperatures will be below freezing and therefore the boat is very dry inside and mould growth is minimal or non-existent. It is best to store cushions standing up to allow air to circulate. All clothes and bedding must be washed - preferably store in plastic bags.

Any foodstuffs or drinks with high water content should be removed.

Sails should be removed and stored in a sail loft if possible or below if no facilities are available.

# APPENDIX V

# SKIPPERS NOTES & PRACTICAL TIPS

**Costs:** Despite the popularly held belief Sweden is not expensive — the exchange rate has made life very much cheaper for Brits. Finland is more expensive than Sweden but is not outrageous compared with UK.

**Alcohol:** In Sweden available only from State shops called Systembolaget — expensive and shops not open at weekends or on public holidays. In Finland state shops are called Alko but the prices and times of opening are not unreasonable. Alcohol is very cheap in the Baltic States and also reasonably priced in Germany.

**Bread:** Is very expensive in most countries.

**Food:** In the Netherlands they are very conscious of sell-by dates and fresh produce including meat is often sold very cheaply on Saturday afternoons. Food is very cheap in the Baltic States. The low cost of meals and the quality of the food makes eating out economic.

It is possible to purchase nearly all requirements in all the countries visited — the same brands of shampoo, cleaners etc seem quite universal. However, bacon is not to be found in Lithuania and Latvia nor throughout southern Estonia. It is available in Tallinn and throughout Sweden Finland etc.

**Things you need to take:** Ordinary English tea (Earl Grey and flavoured teas are available throughout the countries visited) and mansized tissues — these cannot be found anywhere. Long life milk is not available in Sweden — Finnish milk has reasonable life expectancy and long life is available in the Baltic States.

**Gifts:** Amber jewelry and ornaments, and a range of knitted goods can be purchased cheaply in the Baltic States and make excellent presents.

**Diesel:** Duty free diesel is available at Helgoland, Holtenau (if leaving Germany), tax free red diesel in Estonia and Finland. Tax paid diesel is usually purchased from nearest garage in cans. Words to look out for are Estonia — Kutteoli, Finland (Finnish) - Politoöljy Swedish — Brännolja.

**Spares:** It is advisable to carry spares for the engine, in particular, fan belt, water pump, fuel and oil filters. Lubricating oil tends to be expensive and it is as well to carry enough for two oil changes.

It is worth investing in a stern hook and anchor reel to simplify mooring up.

**Know the weight of your boat:** The question is sometimes asked when entering countries but it is mainly necessary if you have to be craned out — remember the gear on board makes a boat much more than the manufacturer's specified weight.

**Money matters:** Credit cards are not often accepted in Germany or even Denmark. Elsewhere most things except harbour fees can be paid for with a credit card. ATMs are common throughout the countries visited so obtaining cash is no problem. Currency exchange is common in the Baltic States — we have found £sterling give a better rate than US$.

**International Camping Gaz:** Is unobtainable in the Baltic States. In Finland refills can be obtained at NJK Yacht Club and in Sweden it has been found in Kalmar, Furusund, Stockholm (Wasahamnen) and at Soderköping (Göta Canal). We have invested in a Swedish bottle and regulator. The alternative is to take Calor propane bottles which can be refilled.

**Access to the Internet:** Available at Public Libraries in Finland and Sweden free of charge for limited periods (usually half an hour). In the Baltic States access is similarly available but for a very small charge.

# INDEX

# INDEX